My Father's Daughter

A Memoir by Shell Norman

Cover Art by Photographer & Graphic Designer, Kevin Carden.

Moral Rights
Shell Norman asserts the moral right to be identified as the author of this work. If you wish to connect with her, find her newsletter @shellnorman.com.

Designators
Names and some details have been changed to protect the privacy of individuals who did not choose to reveal the events described in this story.

Published by *Fire & Feast Books*

First edition

Dedication

For my grandchildren who are here because of my story.

Prologue
Meet Barb

Barb grew up in the south, Betsy Layne, Kentucky, but she's lived in Michigan so long that you can barely detect any of that old southern drawl anymore. Maybe when she refers to her grandmother as "Memaw," you know where she's from. Or when she orders a tea from a nice waitress, she expects that tea to be sweet-iced-tea, low on the ice. . .and the tea.

Barb loved her mom, June, and always honored her too. June raised five kids pretty much alone, three girls and two boys. Before she became an official single mom, she endured frequent beatings from her husband, Jay. He didn't hit the kids as often, but he had no problem showing June who was in charge, and the children certainly witnessed their mom suffer as they stored away video files in their minds saved in a folder called, "Trauma."

Jay filled up most days with Kentucky bourbon, whatever cheap brand he could find. And nights, he would find some cronies out carousing and maybe crash on one of his buddy's sofas if he didn't noisily fiddle with the screen door at home and trip onto his own living room couch.

Back in the '60s, women didn't easily throw a man out, but June finally did. She got herself a shotgun and a restraining order against Jay and then moved her family up north and got a job at a factory in Hazel Park.

She lived her last years in an assisted living complex on the east side, and her grown children visited her often, sitting with her to keep her company or shopping for her favorite little treats. Barb washed her hair and combed a soft conditioner through it on Fridays.

Barb has raised a family of her own with her committed and loving husband, Phil. A complete 180 from her dad. She credits God for allowing that to happen. She says she was lucky to meet a man who knew Jesus, or a boy you might say as they married quite young. He came from a family of faith, and that family, especially Phil's mom and dad, took Barb into a warm shelter.

Barb and Phil attended a little clapboard church house with a crew of married couples raising kids under sound teachings, the likes of Dr. James Dobson. Back then, you might find a dogeared paperback on their table called *Discipline with Love and Logic*. They listened to the gospel songs of The Bill Gaither Vocal Band too, and Phil himself could sing folksy songs in front of the Friday night prayer group, picking his guitar in familiar chord progressions to set the atmosphere. Their three children attended Christian school even though they had to scrape together the funds from a one-income household.

Barb was breaking the family cycle, by the strength of The Lord, she would say. In fact, in thanksgiving, she vowed to not even touch alcohol, an extreme prohibition for herself that her friends, like me, teased her about in fun. We had gotten to know each other back when we were raising children together. *You sure you don't need a little visit from Mr. Jack Daniels? He might help you get through these teenaged years with your kids, ya know*, I might joke. Barb was not easily offended and laughed along with me, no temptation ever putting up a substantial fight.

Not all of Barb's siblings grabbed hold of her faith. She is still close to them and tries to be a good sister and aunt to their kids, but they don't want any Bible-thumping coming their way, and Barb respects that. Her three children grew into nice adults, all productive and in secure relationships. "What a blessing," Barb always says, lifting her hand in praise.

Sitting across from each other in our favorite Middle Eastern restaurant, as we have often done in our thirty-plus years of friendship because we both happen to love a fresh Fattoush salad, Barb blurts out a declaration:

"Have I got a story for you! Just wait till you hear this," she says as I swallow a bite of the tangy sumac covering the pita chips, the best part of the salad.

"*This* is a family secret I never in a million years expected."

I sipped my iced tea to sort of brace myself. I could tell this would be a big one. And I had a secret of my own feeling about the size of a watermelon in the pit of my belly at this point. Those experiments you might have seen online where people put rubber band after rubber band around the melon waiting for the pressure to finally make it explode come to mind. This story might just be the last band.

"So," Barb began "This man, about sixty years old, knocked on my brother's door and said he's our brother. Well, half anyway. My brother was sort of curious and decided to let him tell his story. He believed him right away. Apparently, my father got a young girl pregnant back in the 60s when he was still married to my mom. Sounds like something he would do," she says rolling her eyes. "I guess that's why the guy is believable. This girl was forced to give the baby boy up for adoption, and he grew up with his adoptive parents—in a stable home, Thank God. Now his parents are both passed, and he did DNA testing on one of those sites and somehow found my brother. I guess my brother must have done it too sometime. Not sure how all that works."

This all spills out rather rapidly with Barb's hand gestures revealing a little case of the nerves.

"Did you know any part of this story before? Do you think your mom knew anything about this child?" My voice is a little shaky. Careful. Not as reactive as Barb might expect, and this surprises her a bit. I can see it in her eyes. I'm holding myself together thinking of the anxiety that has been growing inside me for twenty years of sifting through murky water.

"Well," she says. "I remember something from when I was very young. . . the police came to our house one time to pick up my dad, maybe for questioning. All these years, I just dismissed it as something to do with him being drunk and doing something stupid, like hitting a car or something. But now that I think of it, I recall them talking about an 'underage' girl. But he never went to jail or anything, so I don't know. Definitely could have been this incident. Anyway, this guy wants to meet all of the siblings now. He never had any brothers or sisters, or any blood relatives at all, so he really wants to connect with us. My sister already agreed. She wants me to go with her."

I'm sweating around the collar of my blouse and trying to loosen it somewhat.

"I don't want to," she emphatically declares.

"What if it's not even true? What if he's a werido? Do I want to force some sort of relationship with him? Can you ever imagine something like this happening? What would *you* do?"

I'm definitely calmer than Barb expects at this news. I've had a few years to wonder about the whole DNA phenomenon popular these days. I had grown suspicious over the years about surprise relatives I might find, knowing from a young age that it was a possibility that my dad might have another family out there somewhere. And then with my mom springing another secret on me later in life, I avoided the topic of family background all together. I have been hearing stories about people discovering new relatives, and while it can be intriguing, like all those advertisements portray, I know it sometimes doesn't go as planned. I have never mentioned my family's sordid history to Barb before, even though we have been close for thirty-five years, but truth is, I am sort of afraid of those DNA stories. We tend to want to keep the kinds of secrets they could reveal wrapped up tight, hidden in the back of closets under old blankets nobody ever uses. Maybe Barb could be braver than I and untie some of those old ghosts.

Maybe she's more resilient than I have felt lately. I think about that time in my early teen years when my classmate, Leanne, and I were walking home from school atop the frozen Rouge River and the ice broke beneath Leanne. She plunged into the freezing water, up to her waist and then, immediately, shot right back up to the icy floor next to me. We stood shocked for a moment and then continued our brisk walk home before her clothes might freeze and cause her legs to be too difficult to move. Somehow, I am thinking of Barb here, falling through the ice but quickly climbing right back out, continuing her walk on solid ground. She seems the type who could do this.

"Well, what is the harm in meeting him?" I lay that question on the table for her to mull over.

"I don't know," she says. "It just opens up all these doors to memories I can do without. I go through my life day to day not really thinking much about my past, or my dad for that matter. Those early years do not provide many happy memories really. A lot of darkness back there, so do I need to face a person who can light it all up again? Even if he is a brother?"

"Let me take a minute to think," I say as I excuse myself for a break in the restroom.

Would I want to meet a new brother? Should I let all my secrets out, all the anxiety I'm so good at hiding, I wonder?

How very strange that I have been able to keep my past hidden for so long while Barb has skeletons in her closet we've never discussed as well. How many others must be hearing this same rattling of old bones? I certainly won't discuss my worries now no matter what because that seems insensitive to the story she just shared so freely and vulnerably. I'm not a "me monster" trying to top Barb's story with a better one of my own. I just need to be a friend at this point. I sit back down in front of Barb, resigned.

"Okay, so I think you should do it. I think you meet this guy on your own terms. Don't go with your sister; drive your own car so if you are uncomfortable in any way, you can just

10

leave. He does not have to know your address or anything, and you are not 'forced' into a relationship. You are just meeting him. That's all. See what happens from there."

"I guess you're right," Barb says as she prepares to switch topics. "Maybe I will. I'll keep ya posted."

She readjusts herself. "So, tell me about your writing group. I didn't know you were writing a book. Whatever made you decide to do that? And what's it about?"

All loaded questions. I feel that last rubber band stretch around my secrets.

"Well, how about you be one of my beta readers?" Barb is an avid reader, so I would trust her opinion on my writing no matter the topic. But now? Now the topic's a little more close to home. "I will send you a copy of my book in progress, and you will then see why I was compelled to write it. I guess I just *had* to tell my story. I think it will become clear, and my hope is that it reaches others and maybe helps in a way."

"I'm happy to be a 'beta reader,' or whatever you call it. I can't wait."

In the days that follow, I expect my text messages to blow up. I expect quite a reaction from Barb once she begins reading. Here is the first: "SHELL! No way. I can't stop reading. WHAT? How have I known you this long and never really *known* you?"

Part I

You who planted for years in a ground that

Was me

Remain to toil

Gardeners leave seeds in fertile soil

1

My Reflection

On a typical morning, I examine my face in the mirror looking for all the ways it is responding to the aging process. For about twenty years, I have strived to find traits of my father etched in the lines that just keep morphing me closer to my mother's likeness. Nowhere is my dad's rich, dark, thick hair. Mine has always clung to my face lifelessly in a dull, dirty blond. Those Mediterranean, heart-shaped lips skipped over my DNA as well, leaving me with a nearly invisible outline of a mouth that I must chase after and pin down with some Clinique lip liner.

Relatives have always commented on how much little Shelly resembles her mother, Doris, named after a radio actress, Doris Weston, though mom liked to say she was named after the beautiful Doris Day. And, growing up, I was always okay with taking after my mom. She was pleasant looking enough. I could be content to carry on her image, even as I may have sometimes wondered just where my dad dwelled in my reflection.

Throughout my childhood, my mother often pointed out what she deemed were those Italian characteristics inherited from my dad, like my olive skin tone, for example. That tanned skin covered a scrawny little girl who never could eat enough to fill out into my own until well into adulthood. And since years ago, on a winter day in the January after my dad passed away when my mom admitted to her long-hidden affair back in the 1960s, I have struggled to see any of those said Italian traits in myself. Although Doris assured me with one hundred percent certainty that my dad *was* indeed my biological father, the doubts crept in like slow growing cancer, a monster gnawing away my trust in her word.

Small surges of joy and relief have sprung up here and there when a cousin on my dad's side might note how closely our two daughters resemble each other. Or a sibling might remark that my feet are just the same shape as our dad's. Even my sense of humor has echoes of my dad's wit, not at all like my mom's more boisterous behavior. Yet my features . . . my features are not Italian. The sparks of hope always ended up sputtering out.

Twenty years of knowing this little secret of my mother's began to cultivate an insidious suspicion, and suspicion does not mingle well with health. I met Anxiety for the first time as I neared my fiftieth birthday, and she isn't nice.

2

A Forest of Our Own

Growing up in Detroit, my memories are surprisingly not urban at all. New acquaintances at my private high school twenty minutes into a suburb outside of the city would routinely ask me if I ever witnessed a shooting. *Was our house ever burglarized? Do car chases keep us up at night?* I laughed off those questions with a dismissive shrug and never admitted that my dad *did* leave a loaded shotgun tucked into the corner of the hallway, upright and easy to grab, for me on the occasions that I was left home alone at night. He also taught me how to use it. I could hit the bullseye on a target like many teenage boys of that era. Dad advised me: *If you do have to shoot someone trying to get into the house, make sure you drag him all the way in before you call the police so you don't get in trouble.* I think he winked because we both knew I certainly had no such strength for that.

Ironically, we lived in front of a vast wooded parcel of preserved land. The yards to our houses backed up to a field and, then farther back, to timbered trails winding deep into a forest of our own surrounding The Rouge River and little swamps here and there. My childhood was filled with imaginative play. Television was reserved for a few shows aired on about three different channels, but I rarely cared to indulge. Why would I want to stay in and watch *Brady Bunch* when the neighborhood parents allowed us kids to play in the woods all day long? My mom never knew how far into those trails we wandered. One of my favorite little friends, Krissy, lived down the street, and her parents frequently, on weekends when they were free, took us neighborhood kids on two-hour hikes around one side of the woods, telling stories along the way. We would pick up the best walking sticks to tote along with us and then save somewhere secreted away in the yard for another time. We had quite the collection piled up as we always picked a new stick for each walk. That habit stuck with me, and visitors to my home today will see a little pile of thick branches leaning in the corner of my garage, waiting for the perfect walk, as if I need a cane these days.

Krissy and I would stay and play, long after the parents went inside. What we called "witch's hair" hung from bushes throughout the wooded area. This straggly brush proved perfect for concealing forts once we covered the witch's hair with old, fallen leaves. Sometimes we would dig shallow pits into the soft ground, drape the thick witch's hair over the top, and throw the natural mulch all around the surroundings so that nobody walking past would ever find our hiding places. My playmate and I even pretended we possessed good witch's magic too. Some of the kids thought we took our imagination too far in that realm.

Huge boulders marked certain points along the trails in no definitive pattern that we could decode, and we wove stories about old natives placing them there before the neighboring towns were developed. Those rocks spawned taller tales upon each passing. I firmly believed that tiny fairies would sneak out on the velvety, green moss that grew on the damp surfaces. My dad told us that if we could get out to the rocks early enough, like when the sun was just offering the first glimpses of light but not yet warm enough to burn away the morning fog, we would see the fairies dancing, silently tapping their toes on the spongy moss in child-like pliés and twirls, emitting sparkly dust in their wake, blowing and swirling like light, fresh snow. I know I saw them once. And it is a happy memory.

Our favorite destination to our walks was the old fire pit that had not been used in who knows how long. According to our thoughtful calculations, not since the Native Americans inhabited our small forest. Strangely, no one else ever visited these spots or interrupted our reverie, so they became our own historical landscapes. We sat around this twelve-by-twelve circular pit in the middle of the woods, chewing the lemony clover from clusters reaching up through the cracks in the rock and telling stories of ancient plays performed there. We knew our imagined scenarios must be true because the slate that framed the pit was layered upward, like stepping-stone bleachers. To this day, I still wonder who really placed them in such a design, and why else but to perform. I fancy holding on to my theories dreamt up long ago. Like an illustration inked into an old book, I can still envision ancient settlers leaning back against those steps on a summer evening for some entertainment after long days of hard work building strong shelters in preparation against Michigan winters. Maybe chewing on sprigs of long, seeding grass. Krissy's dad named those "Spooksicles," and the natives would have needed a good supply stacked up to ward off any evil spirits.

Nearby, a tall, grey sycamore grew above the tops of the other trees, and if we craned our necks, we could see carvings all the way to the top. The strange markings that had turned black with time frightened us a little because we could not understand the writings of what we determined were ancient hieroglyphics. Only near the bottom did we see the familiar TD + MD kinds of engravings. Dad fed our imaginations with the pretense that he could read a bit of those carvings because his father had long ago shared his own experiences with the natives back in West Virginia.

I could have been a budding writer then. At age nine or ten, I could have told stories of all the pictures in my mind—the hedges that formed a castle's protection, the felled, thick, twisted branches that created a treehouse requiring no additional construction, the abandoned miniature cabin that looked like some sort of dollhouse set alone, deep in those woods. Scurrying up those meandering tree trunks and perching above the dollhouse, we would catch a glimpse of its surroundings from afar. We children had played the story of *Hansel and Gretel* on 33 rpm record albums so often that none of us were ever brave enough to inch right up to the building and peer into the cracking, framed window of that vacant shack, but we did watch the chipmunks from a safe distance hunched on the doorstep hastily gnawing a snack with a confident disregard for human presence.

I had such a connection to nature then—an escape from a reality that was a little too harsh for my young mind. I relate to Ruthie, a character in Marilynne Robinson's *Housekeeping*—a novel that I read back in high school. One of those that cultivated my love of reading and planted the truth that our memory of events from our youth *is* reality for us. That reality shapes who we become.

The landscape of my history always provided a plethora of images I choose to recall even today, edging out the darker images of disputes between my parents or uncomfortable family get-togethers when too much alcohol spilled over onto everyone's behavior. My time in the woods created a world where I preferred to store my memories—the ones that made me who I became in adulthood. It is unnerving when a sure-footed reality dissipates like the lifting of that thick morning haze—when you question who you always thought you were.

3

Stormin' Norman

Rooted and flourishing throughout this landscape was Norm, my father, known affectionately by some as "Stormin' Norman." An outdoorsman who planted this love of nature in me like only a master gardener can. We had the expected father-daughter differences, of course. I was into stories and imaginative play, while dad lived on the tangible—blue collar labor, hunting and fishing. Later, the university called to me. Dad cautiously encouraged me to pursue higher education despite his fear, drilled into him by the rhetoric of his time, that as a woman who deeply desired a family, I might not use a college degree. He paid for it anyway. And I did use it, much to his delighted surprise.

The connection that strung us together beyond any differences was so tight that even now, long after his death, I still experience ethereal visits with him where our conversations make surprisingly good sense, not the usual nonsense typical of dream scenarios. In these places, he stands strong, minus his familiar chronic, phlegmy cough that I had grown up used to hearing. A long-term effect of wounded lungs left over from a near-fatal, childhood illness. His eyes, glassy and green. Not like the color of emeralds but of a murky Lake Erie, matching the camouflage he frequently wore for his hunting trips deep into the woods. And in these visions, he proudly shows me his now-healed body so I do not have to picture him atrophied and gaunt, the condition he was in during the months leading to his death, as he had fought a harrowing war against sepsis.

When the human body is septic, every organ is affected, including the skin, which is simply one large, stretched organ that encapsulates the rest. Normally, we proceed with delicacy when someone has an injured appendage of some sort, but the skin does not always look diseased, yet even in a coma, my father recoiled under the slightest touch to this largest organ. From an undetected ruptured appendix, poison coursed through his bloodstream and invaded every part of him, shutting down kidneys and lungs and stopping all digestion in its tracks. The skin, with its millions of nerve endings, felt the brunt of this poison's punch. Desperately wanting to rub my dad's head or hold his hand to comfort him, we dared not, or we would witness his severe writhing and contortions as reminders. In addition, nurses had his arms strapped to his sides so he would not inadvertently yank out his breathing tube and IV, a common practice for all patients in his condition, but perhaps a little more important for my dad who thrashed violently against anyone coming near him trying to soothe his fears. We were soldiers wanting to protect and guard but told to stand down.

He had barely survived this ordeal, but he did come out of the initial fight ready to rebuild. We began making plans for his return home from the rehabilitation center in Ann Arbor to renewed relationships with those whom he had lost touch. Even talked about attending a church, as long as we warned the parishioners ahead of time that the roof might cave in upon his entrance. Prior to this brush with death, any hope in a higher power had evaded my dad since the time he last served the elements at the altar back in the 1940s. His heart, hardened toward spiritual things, had only a few crevices open that I inhabited, knowing he loved me yet would never fully surrender to my faith, a faith I had cultivated since my teenage years.

I was used to his frequent Archie Bunker type slurs and bigotry against anyone different from him and determined that he used these phrases, perhaps, as masks hiding something deeper. Dark memories of his childhood, maybe. I had long ago given up my indignant reactions of, "D-a-a-a-d! How could you say that!" because I found that my response only brought on more intense declarations, just to get a rise out of me. Broken relationships, illicit other affairs, alcohol abuse and long hours on the road had beaten him down. He had stopped even reaching for hope long before this time. I always knew I could never reform him but rested in our genuine relationship as it was. I was not ready for it to end here, though.

But then he woke from his septic shock reflecting a man who had just about touched the face of God. A new man. A peace that escaped explanation. Also exhibiting a new-found appreciation for my mother who had stood by his side with an uncharacteristic tenacity I never realized she possessed, refusing to let him go. Norm desperately expressed a desire to reabsorb some missed sunshine and breathe in the fresh air wafting around the acreage on which his own newly built house waited for him.

Alas, his heart gave up the fight without his soul's consent, and Norm never made it home.

How we longed for just a little more time. Time of normalcy where dad would call for us to join him searching the dirt roads around his home to see if he could help us find new plots of land as he planted the dream of moving our family out his way too, like my brother had. My brother, Ricardo, lived across about 50 acres from my parents and was on his way to raising his own kids to appreciate nature as much as their grandfather did. My mom sold that property soon after dad passed, as it was never her dream to live out in the country. And my brother soon left the area too. It is quite a trek these days to visit the gravesite of my parents as we have no other excuse for heading out that way. Dad's prediction that he would lay at rest under that towering oak tree with no visitors coming to talk came true as he never knew the kind of families that visited gravesites much, so he didn't suspect that we would be any different. I planned to visit often if only to prove dad wrong about that, but years surely go by without a stop at that old cemetery. I find myself talking to mom or dad in the middle of the night during that time between wakefulness and sleep. Better conversations occur there than standing in front of a quiet, granite stone. He seems to understand, and I catch a little smile before the image disappears.

4

Spiraling Around My DNA

Even though Norm was partial to dogs growing up and called all our cats "fleabags," he was a gentle animal lover. He would often threaten to get rid of the cats that always seemed to follow my sister home from school by "taking them for a ride" and dumping them off somewhere, but he never actually did. Never could he get himself to carry out the heartless threat. When he did not hear me come into the living room once, I caught a glimpse of him stroking the fur of our seemingly-always-pregnant cat, named Charlie for her Charlie Chaplain style markings in black and white and for, early on, mistaking her for a male cat. Thinking he was alone, he used the higher pitched baby talk voice typically reserved for cats versus dogs. He would never admit to such affection toward Charlie, especially since she delivered litters of kittens too often in her lifetime, all for which we had quite the struggles finding homes. While pretending she was a nuisance, he always saved the innards of whole chickens for her, cutting up liver and kidney parts into tiny cubes and putting them aside for her bowl while he cooked a meal for our family.

On every family vacation driving down south or out west, my dad would stop for breaks at a deer farm or nature reserve so we could get out of the car, stretch our legs and go feed, and maybe even pet, some wildlife. Most of the home movies I have since had transferred from 8 mm to DVD are of us at various preserves with moose, elk, bear, and birds of prey. So often when we were young, we would beg daddy to show us the home movies projected on the wall, and we'd bust out laughing at the goat that butted my sister in the rear or the giant goose that stole the ice cream cone right out of my little hands. We would munch on the popcorn dad made using a little oil in the medium Farberware saucepan. A generous sprinkle of salt, and butter heated in the still-hot pan poured over top. Maybe some Pepsi to wash it down. Dad would have to splice back the singed, melting film several times throughout movie night and open the window to let the smell of burnt plastic escape.

Once my parents moved out to the more rural area outside of Detroit, it was a welcome pastime to pile into the mint green Aerostar around dusk to go deer spotting, never to discuss any thrill-of-the-kill hunters might share but, instead, to just enjoy watching the animals in their natural habitat.

I saw a few deer on someone's property one night helping themselves to the farmer's crop, and I asked dad what they were eating. Dad responded as if delivering a punchline, right on cue: "Some poor bastard's beans." A little iced tea I had just sipped from an uncovered plastic cup sprayed out of my nose. Caught off guard, we all cracked up and have since filed that phrase in a metaphorical folder we call "Normisms."

Inevitably, I'd have to go to the bathroom, especially since we always brought those drinks with us on our adventures. Mom often said I must have an infant sized bladder. From a very young age, I was used to going in the woods behind a tree, unlike today's youth who might be horrified at the idea. On one occasion, I asked dad to pull over. Now that I was an adult, I searched for a little more privacy to relieve myself.

Dad found the perfect spot—a dilapidated, abandoned trailer, half on its wheels and half off. I would just run behind the tin structure and take care of my issue and run back to the van real quick since it was rather cold out that evening. As I was indisposed, sort of leaning against the trailer, I got the fright of my life. An old man, and when I say old, I mean one who looked embalmed, gray and skeletal, popped up in front of the window and saw more than he bargained for. I screamed and ran back to the car without zipping up, jumped in and dad peeled off the property with the squeals of laughter on high volume for what seemed like the rest of the drive.

On all of our leisurely drives, I never minded the faint smell of tobacco as my dad rested his arm on the open window ledge, holding his cigar half in and half out of the minivan, a trail of smoke circling to the backseat where I breathed in a bit of its essence and let it mingle with the grass and trees that would offer the most powerful fragrance.

I was his best deer spotter. The one to find them first, winning some unnamed contest as I watched him smile at my talent—the keen sight over the field grass and between tall tree trunks almost the same tawny color as the animals themselves.

Dad's demeanor always calmed from the day behind him at the time, and he exuded a palpable serenity out in the woods. Perhaps I got this appreciation from him—the ability to find peace out in nature. When I need to escape whatever variety of current tensions plague me, that's where I go.

As I walk along a forest trail, the burdens of the day or the week start sloughing off and decomposing on the path behind me. I'll close my eyes and listen to a sparrow's twittering. The breeze will massage my shoulders, and I'll feel lighter in my steps, sort of bouncing along rather than lugging myself to the end of the path. Here I connect with both my creators: my earthly father *and* the spiritual—my Holy Father. Here, I pray.

And when I feel memories of Norm slipping away with time, I walk through the woods, inhaling deep breaths to awaken those sleepy thoughts. Lilies of the Valley, pine needles, dewy grass, damp wood all take me back to a solid ground and center me.

And I can feel my dad here. I am not connected with anyone else in this way.

Those memories and connections are rooted deep within. Spiraling around my DNA.

5

You Were Not a Mistake

My mom was a fun-loving sort, just not toward my dad for most of their marriage. The sound of her laughter can barge into my memories and cheer me at times all these years after her death, like the trill from the cardinals she often imitated. Doris was a strong, athletic type, confidently sporting her sparse, bottled auburn hairdo teased up once a week at the local beauty shop and protected each night with strips of toilet paper wrapped tightly around the updo. God forbid, dad would ever splash that hair in the backyard pool on those rare occasions we were all in it together.

She could be blunt, but people found this endearing and sometimes funny. Growing up, our relationship was good, except for the one demon that wedged between us and held us at a comfortable arms' length much of my youth. She believed her whisky and diet 7-UP was her only reliable friend in life, the one whom she could lean on and trust to be there for her, perhaps to hold onto her greatest secret, for she never divulged her main indiscretion in all my years prior to that January day in the second half of my adulthood.

Doris had no talent for chicanery, but not for lack of trying. She was not morally above deception; secrets just found a way to bust out, revealing themselves in her expressions before she thought to reel them back in for safekeeping. She had a tell, and no ability to conceal that tell ever prevailed. My mom divulged too many things, even about my dad—intimate details no daughter would ever want to hear. Or about a certain family member who found herself pregnant from her very new boyfriend. Though mom was sworn to secrecy about the relative's imprudence, she was the first to relay such news to me despite my pleading with her to stop before it all fell out in too many pieces to pick up and shove back in.

Although she loved having a story to tell and enjoyed watching the reactions to her minor embellishments, she knew that some people placed a level of importance on the keeping of a secret. But storytelling for an audience was a temptation she could not resist. So many times, we heard the story of how, with a metal spatula, she beat up a man who threatened her at a Mic Mac picnic, and every time she relayed the incident, the man had bled more from the cut straight down the middle of his bald head.

She also felt she *deserved* to know certain things, like the fact that her friend's husband was sleeping with his secretary, or that our neighbor had eyes for her and almost acted upon his desires while his own wife was otherwise engaged. And somehow, she thought *I* might like to know these things too. Even at a young age, I metaphorically plugged my ears, especially when it came to hearing of my dad's failures. I think it irked her that her revelations about him did not taint my view of him. She wondered how I could love him as much as I did despite all the ways he came up short for her.

Resentment toward my father's and my relationship broke soil when I was about ten. I couldn't have named it then, but I felt something uncomfortable from the cold looks or the tsk-tsking I heard as she would often turn a different direction, sip her brown, icy drink and mutter quietly when my dad and I were laughing about something she didn't think was very funny. Since my parents were always standing dangerously close to that cliff near divorce, about to take a flying leap, I never imagined they would stay together until the end or that mom would be a bed-side warrior pulling my dad back to life, though briefly, during his final illness. Despite knowing they each loved me in their own ways, I always knew that my birth was a complication in their muddy lives. I just didn't know quite how muddy it all was.

My mom let it slip once that she contemplated abortion when she found herself pregnant with me—a predicament that both surprised her and infringed on her plans. She thought she was leaving my dad until this revelation. They had the money in the 1960s that would allow her to have the procedure done safely, if not sympathetically, in an actual hospital, and she was never afraid of any rumored health risks from this *operation*, as she called it, having experienced other surgeries with only jagged yet painless scars to mark them. And she didn't hold fast to any moral grounds at this time, especially without the modern technology of ultrasounds depicting pictures of something other than a clump of cells growing inside. She already had her two children in the 1950s when it was appropriate and she was moderately, happily married, at least outwardly, for I don't really retain many examples of happily married couples of that era, in my world anyway. In fact, my parents struggled quite a bit back then to even get pregnant with my brother and sister as they had a couple of fertility strikes against them.

How many times had I heard the description of my dad's sperm? Not the kind of conversation typical for a mother and her young child to be sure, but I knew from as early as I can remember that it took six years of trying with my mom's first pregnancy. My parents would have to collect my dad's semen in a Mason jar, and mom would carry it against her chest to keep it warm as they drove it to the clinic. One time, the doctor invited them to view a sample under a microscope. Normal sperm swam and flitted about vigorously, but Norm's had motility issues. The tiny swimmers were all sluggish and quickly vanquished. Nevertheless, the doctor would insert the sample into Doris and wait for some good news. How many times they did this procedure over the years, I do not really know. Couple this problem with the fact that my mom had also experienced a previous tubal pregnancy and had had to have her right-side ovary and fallopian tube removed, so the chance of viable eggs only likely occurred during half of her cycles. But finally, my sister, Antoinette, was conceived. And two years later, my brother, Ricardo, came along. They had never used birth control methods to stop pregnancy since their chances for success were always so slight anyway. After many years had passed, the last pregnancy would definitely come as a surprise.

Apparently, my dad talked Doris out of terminating the pregnancy, and after suspicions and accusations about where this baby came from ten years after the first two, they fell back into the appearance of married life and went on as if I were a pleasant and welcome third child. Turns out I was. I never minded that I was "an accident." I thought it was mighty lucky I ended up here, and I tried to convince my mom that I was okay with the knowledge of my accidental status, but she would have none of that.

"You were *not* an accident," she'd say with mock indignation, forgetting her little admission that had escaped in the past about wanting to end that pregnancy. "You were just unexpected. We always knew we wanted three children; we just didn't think it would happen after how difficult it was to have the first two, and then you came along. Meant to be. We hoped it would be sooner, but I guess the man upstairs had different plans bringing you to us."

But I knew that *unexpected* was the same thing as accidental, and I also knew that my sister was the one who named me Michelle instead of the expectant parents choosing a name. Back then, I didn't often question why they didn't come up with a name that meant something to them, perhaps in homage to a family member. Something Italian, like Sofia or Isabella. Even my sister garnered the nickname, Toni, in honor of both of her grandfathers named Anthony but always called Tony. Many times, I heard my mom's rendition of how my conception happened: right before the uncharacteristically spontaneous act of intercourse, for them at least, she'd cautioned my dad,

"If we don't want any more children, shouldn't we use some protection?"

And Norm's answer was, "Oh you can't get pregnant after all this time!" Mom would end this often-repeated account the same every time:

"And sure enough, right after that, I turned up pregnant." Familiar chortle following.

She kept trying to assure me that I was not a mistake.

6

Torn in Half

Despite the initial, unwelcome arrival of a young child in their tumultuous marriage, I *did* know I was wanted later. Contrary to what a counselor once harshly told me, that my parents did not truly love me, I knew they did love me, even if through a haze of self-focused, often drunken states of parenthood.

One time, they physically fought over me. Mom had gotten fed up with something and abruptly dragged me into the car to run away with me. However, this happened after imbibing too much diet soda and Corby's to be driving down our twisting neighborhood street, or anywhere for that matter.

Dad quickly chased us in his car and caught up. He jumped out and opened my passenger side door, grabbing my arm against the pull of my mom's grasp on the other arm as the car continued slowly rolling down the road, dad jogging alongside, yelling.

"Don't take her. You can't drive—you'll hurt her, damn it."

Both yanked and screamed above my rather quiet and dumbfounded whimpers. The danger of ripping apart like the alleged child in front of Solomon's wise judgment, while crossing my mind now, didn't come up at the time, of course. What I was left with was that they both wanted me. I don't remember who let go.

Psychology tells us this is not love, but I didn't know any better. It *was* somehow.

When I was about five years old, on a very rare occasion, the family was sitting around the dinner table together, and I unwittingly decided to hug Slicker, our rotund, tricolored beagle, while he was begging for food. After an uncharacteristic growl erupted from the dog's throat, my mom mistakenly attempted to discipline the dog without removing me from the situation first.

Slicker lurched at my face and caught my lip just under my nose, biting right through. My mom knew it was her fault and felt horrible. She shook her head to flick off the annoying tears so she could see better as she cradled me in her lap, pressing a wadded towel to sop up the blood while my dad ran down the basement after his shot gun. He planned to plainly shoot the dog right there in our dining room as my sister screamed,

"No, daddy, No. Please don't kill him!"

Amidst crying, shouting and pleas for the dog's life, my dad said he would let me decide the fate of Slicker, the beloved family pet.

I saved his life, obviously, and while this seems like a violent reaction in today's world, it was quite normal in our world. In Norm's logic, no animal's life took precedence over his little girl's pain or scarring.

I wasn't mad at my dad, nor did I ever think it was strange that he would have killed our dog if I let him. I just knew he wanted to protect me at all costs. He continued to love on this beagle for years after this incident.

In a cute little game played with the dog, dad would lie on the living room floor and, with a funny dog-talking voice, question Slicker over and over.

"Did you bite Michelle? Did you bite Michelle?"

And the dog would act embarrassed, tail between his legs, and lay his neck over my dad's face, covering his mouth and muffling his words as if he couldn't bear to hear them. My mom retold this story to friends many times admitting to her own guilt in it, and my dad never made her feel bad about it.

With death, some of the negative memories have dissipated like ghosts, following close behind the bodies into the ground. If I call them up, I know there were times when I pretended not to see my parents drinking themselves into a stupor. Especially at gatherings with friends or in front of others, for instance.

On one family vacation, I sat with some young teenagers around the motel's pool deck while my parents sat across the pool socializing in the only way they knew how. When it was time for the adults to head in and search for some sleep, my dad could hardly walk. I tried to ignore the struggle Doris was having, letting my dad lean on her and climb the outdoor steps to the motel room, wobbling at every turn. The young people were distracting enough that I could keep the conversation going and hope that they wouldn't notice my embarrassment, talking louder by the minute to keep their attention to our group. That strategy was not successful for long as one of the more muscular guys sitting near me popped up and ran to help my mom as both were in danger of falling down those concrete steps by this point. Of course, I had to follow. Even in my teenage selfishness, I certainly did not want them to get hurt, so I sheepishly expressed my appreciation for this act of kindness.

Dad was safely deposited onto the bed, and I could slink back down to the pool, feigning indifference to the situation in front of the others.

Dad was usually just a sleepy drunk, and I could handle that a little more easily than I tolerated my mom's tendency to say some intense things when she spent too much time with that favorite liquid friend of hers. Sometimes she would glare at me with eyes that bore right through me. I did not know then that it could have been a deep, dark secret she was tying up inside with the strongest restraints she could find. I just knew I would have to turn away and leave the room to escape those moments.

I much prefer to revel in the more pleasant memories I collect like playing cards, trying to stack a good hand. Memories of mom weeding around our above-ground pool in the summertime with one of her ducklings she captured from the woods or from the golf course. Since the duckling inevitably imprinted on her, it always followed closely behind, peeping and waddling along, catching the earthworms mom threw to the side as she worked.

She took pride in her planted spider flowers, cleome hassleriana they are officially called, decorating the perimeter of our very small yard in Detroit. Dad took her shopping at local nurseries each spring to procure vegetable seeds and flowers for the yard. We snapped a photograph each year of her standing next to her towering, giant caster bean plant at the front of the house. The yellow rose bush planted by the side door of our little ranch bloomed faithfully each year as it rebelled against winter. Mom could not leave that bush when they sold and moved out to the country in the '80s. So Dad dug it up for her and planted it snugly against the new house in out in the country, and, surprisingly, she bloomed happily there too as if to say thank you for bringing her along.

It's not so hard to believe that after my parents' death, I again dug up this rose bush and planted her at my own house. She remained a friend for years, waving with soft summer breezes and reminding me of the better parts of home on that sweet plot of land in front of the woods.

7

Smacking Face-First into a Tree

Toni and Rikky grew up so fast I could hardly catch them long enough to record many memories. I dig through childhood and unearth a few from before they moved out and left me more like an only child at home. My brother, Ricardo, was a dare devil. A thrill seeker from an early age. And with the woods being our playground, he had every opportunity to try out his tricks, like the time he was high in a treehouse pulling up five-year-old me with a rope tied around my waist. Just as my mom came looking for me, she caught him and demanded he lower me before I reached the top and stood precariously on this unguarded platform from which I could not survive a fall.

I do not even have an accurate count for how many broken bones Rikky suffered or how many lacerations he had repaired. I do remember him at the tender age of thirteen attaching a rope quite high between two tall maples in the woods behind our house. He had found a handle piece of an old pulley system and decided to test it out, unattended by adults. After climbing up, up, up, still higher in the tree, grabbing the pulley's handlebars he had haphazardly thrown over the rope, he took a flying leap, attempting to swing from one tree to the other like the Tarzan character he watched faithfully in the late '60s TV series.

Unfortunately, the rope broke, and my brother slammed into the tree on the other side that had stood firm, just daring him. In addition to breaking his arm and severely scraping his skin in various places, he knocked out his front teeth too. I'm sure he procured a concussion as well, but I do not remember that diagnosis as I was just a little girl at the time.

Strangely, the Fletchers, the neighbors who collected his crumpled body from the grass below and took him into their house, did not call an ambulance. They did, however, call my dad at work and tend to Rikky while they waited for dad to arrive. I happened to be playing at their house with their young daughter, Maryann. And while they would not let us see my brother, we could hear his frightening moaning from the room across the hall, and that was the only confirmation that he was still alive. What we did see was multiple trips down the short hallway to the one bathroom in the back of the house where Mrs. Fletcher carried full pots of blood and poured them down the toilet, flushing at the same time to prevent overflow.

Soon my dad arrived. Serious, hushed conversation drifted down the hall, my dad's voice gentle and comforting. I remember tentatively peeking around the opening of the doorway to the room where my little friend and I had been sequestered. My dad had my brother in his arms all wrapped up like a small mummy, my brother exclaiming, "My teeth. My teeth." My dad, probably thinking that's the least of our worries here, instead, reassured him, "We'll fix your teeth. Don't worry. Quiet now, Son." Dad winked at me as he hugged Rikky tightly, pulling him close and navigating his body out the front door and into his own car for the short drive to the hospital.

I waited long into the evening before my mom picked me up and took me home. I don't know if my brother stayed overnight at the hospital or came home that night, but I remember mom retelling the story for years afterward, her voice not so unruffled as her fears escaped in harsher tones and judgements, both against my brother's foolhardiness and the neighbors' neglect to call professional help. Rikky had two false teeth placed and body parts fixed, and none of this deterred him from future fearless adventures. How many phone calls my parents must have received over the years as my brother was rushed to the hospital again and again. Bicycle accidents, and later, motorcycle accidents or misfortunate collisions with baseballs or cars all kept my parents on alert, yet they never lost their minds over the possibilities, and Ricardo made it to adulthood, albeit with a permanent limp from a compound fracture of both the tibia and fibula obtained in his early twenties from crashing through the spokes of a dirt bike's wheel. This first scenario, though, archived in my mind since childhood, was an early seed of trust and confidence in my father's care for his children. I never wavered in my faith that my dad would be there for us whenever we needed a sure, calm hand.

They say some people have a natural rhythm and can either dance or not. Sure, you can take a class and learn, but if you are missing that talent, it's very difficult to act it out on the floor.

On the many formal occasions of our lives, like relatives' weddings or golden anniversary parties, my dad never neglected a dance with me, even if he had to carry me. Or, as I grew older, let me step on his feet as he moved to the music.

On my wedding day, I looked forward to that father-daughter dance and chose the obvious: Al Martino's *Daddy's Little Girl*. Snappily dressed, his greying coif greased with precision, my dad enthusiastically stood on the platform and reached out his hand to pull me in tight.

Cheek to cheek, with the smell of Old Spice diffusing the air around us, we listened to the words, dad humming along: *"You're daddy's little girl to have and hold/The end of the rainbow/The pot of gold/A precious gem is what you are . . ."*

And I *was* a treasure to my dad. At least that's what he made me believe, especially as he sang the words along with the crooner. That old-fashioned waltz-like dancing to Big Band music may not be the style these days, but back then, my dad could lead like a professional. Somehow being in his strong embrace and whisked around the dance floor made me feel a most secure confidence. Just like I did as a small child perched on his hip as he swung and twirled me to the music pouring forth from the hi-fi. Music etched on thirty-three speed LPs of Dean Martin or Elvis Presley flowed through those built-in, fabric-covered speakers.

Here, at my wedding reception, I could close my eyes and follow my dad's steps, anticipating his every next move as if I had rehearsed this dance for the stage. As if I knew how to waltz. I don't.

To this day, I cannot follow anyone else, including my own husband of thirty-plus years. My dad is the only one with whom I could ever sync up and appear to have that natural, graceful gift. As if some ancient instinct implanted on our genetic code strung us together like notes on a musical staff, creating a most harmonious melody.

8

You Can't Do That

At about the age of thirteen, I buddied up with a family that attended a full gospel church instead of the Catholic Church our Italian family had settled into, simply by tradition. My parents never practiced, but they sent us kids to the local parish to complete the sacraments. I enjoyed the catechism in my youth, unlike my sister and brother who always skipped out the back door of the school seconds after drop-off at the front and went about their way with like-minded friends. But without the support from parents to reinforce this education, I was easily drawn away to a family that participated in worship services together at this rather rustic, small house in one of the old neighborhoods of Detroit, the house sort of recycled for more spiritual practices. My family could not understand the draw to a ramshackle little church house when the Catholics proudly decorated their cathedrals with elaborate art, and you could count on the aroma of ancient frankincense during meditative prayer, putting you in the proper mood for the liturgy, even though it never worked that way for my siblings. One would assume my chosen path would be the more desirable compared to what I could have fallen into without any moral guidance from home. I was not smoking or stealing or skipping school, but my "churchiness" earned me some teasing from Antoinette and Ricardo, to put it mildly. And, in turn, this alerted my mother to the idea that I was following this other family into what may be at worst a cult and at best, I guess, the land of Jesus freaks.

"Norman, your daughter has left the Catholic Church. Aren't you going to do something about this?"

"She'll figure it out. She's got a good head on her shoulders." He *did* pull me aside and ask if I truly believed in this message enough to change my religion, or if I were simply following this family because of, say, peer pressure, or maybe I was missing something in life, perhaps from his lack of religious encouragement. He thought that could be a real possibility, but he really was not prepared to do anything about it himself. He never attempted to control me in any way, and I appreciated that, but he also wouldn't hear of any "Bible-thumping" directed at him either. He made himself clear that I couldn't expect him to jump on board. It would be a long time before I witnessed the unexpected and completely genuine conversion of my dad before his death.

At some point in my adulthood, I decided that it wasn't so much about my parents' behavior at dinners and other gatherings that I didn't like. It was my own. The fact that they would inevitably drink too much, and I could predict some embarrassing performances, filled me with angst weeks prior to any one event. And this changed my own behavior to the point of stressing out everyone around me. Sometimes I begged a little ahead of time for them to refrain, but to no avail. I came to the conclusion that in order to give up any sort of manipulation of their actions, I could only control my own home. No alcohol allowed in my home anymore. As it was, my parents never visited without a brown bag hiding securely in my dad's jacket for him to pull out at the first opportunity of any conversation poured over ice, in a tall, thin glass. This new decree was drastic, and I actually had to practice informing my family of the new rule, rehearsing the anticipated conversation over and over, gearing up. I would stop asking them to quit. I would stop discussing ahead of get-togethers the dangers of drunk driving or whatever. I would stop worrying. My house would be my haven.

Taking a stroll around my neighborhood one evening with my mom and my sister, I began the rehearsed script, bracing for their reaction that I knew would erupt.

"You can't do that!" My mom said rather loudly while my sister just kind of chuckled under raised eyebrows, as if to say, *Oh yeah? You really think this is going to work with our parents?* Mom sniffed and touched her nose an awful lot. Made that raspberry noise with her lips, but not in fun the way you do with children, blowing out wet judgment. And then Antoinette composed herself to speak her mind carefully.

"I could see if you said no smoking in your house because that stinks, you know, affects your furniture and your clothes and things. But drinking? I'm sure. That doesn't even affect you. You sure you are not just trying to tell us all what to do? You probably shouldn't try to control people, ya know?"

"Oh, but you see, Sis, it does affect me." I kept to my script. "I am letting go of trying to control you. See, I am not trying to tell you not to drink on your own time. You do whatever you want. But if you want to come to my house, that's when you refrain. Otherwise, don't come, I guess."

"Well, your father will not hear of this. He will never come to your house again. Is that what you want?"

"Mom, if dad chooses not to come over, I will keep visiting him. I will still come to your house anytime because if I feel myself getting uncomfortable, I can just leave. It gives

51

me more control over myself is all. This is about me, not you." I tried to keep circling back to that mantra. "It is *my* problem I am working on. I will stop trying to change you. That's a good thing. Be happy about that."

"This is going to make your dad so angry. I can't believe you, of all people, would do that. Wait till I tell him this little plan of yours. He won't agree to this."

"We will just do the family gatherings elsewhere if need be. This way, I can let go of my own anger, and nothing negative will be directed at him." Of course, this cemented her own fury even more. While she outwardly expressed confidence in knowing my dad's reaction, little hidden doubts may have niggled at her. *How would Norm take this news*, she must have wondered.

Mom told Norm the new edict in front of us all, planning for us to witness his reaction. Arms folded in front of her, she blurted out the announcement.

"Michelle has decided that no alcohol is allowed in her home. Like we're all children!" Emphasis on children.

Much to her surprise, my dad answered matter-of-factly, with a shrug of his shoulders, as if he was already prepared for such a declaration: "It's her house. She can do whatever she wants."

My mom reluctantly told me that he never gave her the satisfaction she so fervently desired to be right about his anger. In fact, he dismissed the whole discussion as if it meant absolutely nothing. And soon after, my dad made an hour-long trip to my house in the city by himself. Not something he was in the habit of doing without mom. He came in for a while just to chat. He brought a little stuffed cat and mouse from Arbor Drug Store for my girls, sat on the floor making the cat chase the mouse to the kids' shrieks and laughter, and after a little while, he planted kisses on our cheeks and waved goodbye as he left to run some errands on his way back to his home out in the country. Despite the chilly weather, he came in and out of the house without a jacket, almost to show off the fact that the famous brown bag was missing.

Much later in life, and after both parents had passed, my octogenarian Aunt Celia, my dad's sister, piped up at a family dinner, "I know where you were conceived!" Suspicion had already taken root in my soul and, by this time, had sprouted many shoots in various directions.

"Oh really?" I asked, "Do tell," even though this was an awkward time to bring up such an unsolicited nugget of information.

"Your mom and dad were driving down to Florida taking the mountain roads when they decided to pull over for a little...you know.

So right there in the backseat of their candy-apple red Buick. . ." She went on with a wave of her hand.

"Your mom told me the story, laughing about the irony of getting pregnant so easily when she wasn't even trying. And after all those years of trying so hard with your sister and brother." She shook her head in awe of the story she always remembered. Somewhat of a miracle.

"I guess I heard part of this story before," I said—thinking about the lack of protection comment mom had declared many times. "I just never dreamed it was so spontaneous—in the back seat of the Buick. Knowing my mom, seems she would have enjoyed mentioning that part." We all laughed knowingly.

I never pictured my mom and dad having passion strong enough to pull over to quench some immediate, heated thirst for fulfillment. They always seemed more like annoyed siblings living together than a couple that would make out in the back seat of a car. But what do I know? At least this story pretty much matched my mom's description she had often recounted for me. I liked hearing this version from my aunt and took it as a sign—one of the many I collected through the years, keeping score on one side or the other. Was I my dad's offspring or the result of this affair my mom had back in the 60s?

9

The Act of Washing His Feet

Washing my dad's feet months into his rehabilitation after his appendix ruptured was strangely sacred. Impossible to miss was the ceremonial feel that this act was religious in some way. For many weeks, my dad could not even endure the slightest touch to his skin as his whole body was infected by the poison that coursed throughout threatening to take his life. He had now agreed that it was time to attend to his nails and callused, dead skin, and I was the natural one to take on this task.

This recovery was spiritual as much as physical since Norm credited God for raising him from sure death. A nurse's aide helped me situate his wheelchair into a large space with some supplies—a pan of warm water, ivory soap with a hint of lavender and some soft, cotton towels. The lighting in this room was dim with a few rays of strong sunlight pushing their way through a tall window, and we couldn't help but think of dad's resurrection from this harrowing experience. He was sweetly wistful as he watched me carefully wipe his feet. I was experienced with this gentle touch as my dad had always suffered from bouts of gout and had been commissioning my foot rubs since my early childhood. He must have been reminiscing about all those times in the past that I had helped soothe his pain.

"You know, Sweet Pea," he would often say to me while running his fingers through his thick hair, styled with Brylcreem into the duckbill left over from the 1950s, "the youngest girl in an Italian family can't get married because she has to stay home and take care of her father." I always giggled and said I would still take care of him even if I did get married.

"You always have to be willing to rub my feet for me, especially when I have the gout, but don't you worry too much," he used to say, "I'm not going to live to a ripe old age, so you'll have time to get married after a while." A wet chuckle would escape as every breath mingled with persistent mucus. I really didn't mind this directive whether he meant it or not. His smile and the little twinkle in those large, hazel eyes told me he did not really mean to hold me to it.

He had survived a bad case of both pleurisy and pneumonia as a twelve-year-old, leaving him with these permanently scarred lungs and the chronic cough that sounded like an old engine trying to turn over. His doctor from that time said he wouldn't likely live to see age forty. Hearing that prediction uttered many times when I was perhaps too young to calculate the real odds of overcoming such a prophecy, I often feared his sudden death. Dad even had his burial suit picked out when he was still quite young and healthy, as if this were a normal part of planning ahead. I recall a vivid image of him coming down the escalator at the airport on one of the occasions that mom and I picked him up. This was in the days when you could walk through to the gate to meet your loved ones instead of waiting in the car down by baggage claim. He was wearing a parakeet-blue polyester, two-piece suit, and he sure looked sharp with his hair all slicked into his trademark pompadour. He knew it too. With a smile on his face, he greeted us and, with a quick wave of his hand from top to bottom, instructed, "This is the suit I want to be buried in. Remember that." He was well into his 40s or nearing 50 by then and must have been thinking that he had already passed the prediction and was nearer his expiration date on earth.

Back at that Mic Mac picnic years ago, I am reminded of what started the fight that evoked such violence from my mom, making her go running after a man with a metal spatula in her hand; it was a totally unexpected sucker punch from one of the nearby picnickers straight to my dad's face. One that caught him off guard and clear knocked him out. The image of my father lying on his back, unconscious in a pool of blood has remained vivid since that summer day when I was about six years old. An older teenager from our group whisked me away behind a pavilion to shelter me from the chaos that ensued after the initial punch. I was sure my dad was dead at that point, but before long, he ambled around, searching for me. As soon as he found me and took hold of me under my arms, he gently set me on top of a picnic table to look me straight in the eyes.

"I'm okay, honey. Did you think daddy was dead? I'm right here. I'm okay," he assured as he kissed my forehead, lingering for a moment in comfort. His eye was turning purple, and his nose was still dripping a bit of blood around the tissue stuffed up inside of it, but he smiled with confidence, confirming that he was truly okay. He was strong.

"They can't get rid of me that easy," he joked. And he hugged me tight.

One time, a little later in life, I peered over the deck railings at his house toward his garden and saw the bottom half of his body lying on the ground, half in among the thick corn stalks and half out. I screamed, "D-a-a-a-d" and went running to him, yelling behind me to my mom. "Mom, call for help. Dad's unconscious in the garden!" She didn't move very fast but followed me to the garden with a smirk on her face.

"He's okay. He always is." She waved off the situation with sheer dismissal. "He does that sometimes." Turns out, he liked to lie stomach down while pulling stubborn weeds among his vegetables to avoid his back aching like crazy later. They both just laughed at my concern while my heartbeat slowed back down to normal and I wiped the sweat from my forehead with the back of my hand.

He had beat the odds stacked against him and lived up toward seventy years old, and despite his premonition of an early death, I was becoming hopeful that he would stay around into old age, and if I had to take care of him, I would.

During his frequent reminders, "You are my youngest, and you know what that means," I always just rolled my eyes in fun and continued rubbing those swollen, painful ankles. More times than I can count. And here I was as an adult, married, still rubbing his feet.

Our skin tone matched. I watched my tanned hands rub lotion into those calluses as if they were always meant to do this work. As if I was a part of him. I noticed, even my toes were shaped just like his. The familiarity of those feet and hands are forever imprinted in my mind. I have since learned of "muscle memory." My hands carry the memory of holding my dad's hands. His were scarred by years of sheet metal work and felt rough, like sandpaper. I have never since seen anyone else with such permanent cuts engraved into his hands, but I remember the feel of my dad's never-quite-healed scrapes and sores. I can feel them even now, twenty-plus years after his death. This memory of one of his last days on earth stands firm with its arms folded, facing me, barring my way past it. I could no more fight that memory than I could let my dad slip away from me, no matter how many years pass. He is always standing right in front of me.

Norm's elbows had a tendency toward roughness, what mom labeled as mild psoriasis. I had it too and mom said I inherited that condition. *She* certainly did not have it. What I consider pesky little moles existed in various exposed places on my body too. Most young girls would be self-conscious of these defects, but dad labeled them "beauty marks," and they have forever remained such. Many times, my dad would walk by me and put his arm up next to mine comparing skin tones.

"Don't get any tanner," he'd say, "or you'll pass me up." When others would comment on how the sun always found me, mom would call me a little brown berry.

"That's the Italian blood in her," she would state matter-of-factly for anyone around listening. She also frequently discussed my brother's and my own "Mediterranean anemia," better known today as thalassemia, an inherited disorder sometimes found in people of Italian descent. I don't know that either one of us were ever officially diagnosed with any type of anemia in childhood, but it seemed common knowledge in my household that we both were afflicted by this syndrome. Many years later, my brother mentioned that he had indeed been recently officially diagnosed with thalassemia and had no memory of my mom telling us we had this as children. He actually telephoned to warn me of it, saying I better go get checked out because I may have it too. It would have been passed down by our father, he told me. That could tick one more point on the right side in the tally of my questions of paternity…perhaps. But I am not anemic.

10

Michelle & I Say Goodbye

I have no memory of my mom ever staying overnight anywhere during my childhood, but, of course, one does not have to stay over a whole night to have an affair. My mom had a bowling night on Monday evenings with her friends and a golf night on Fridays. And she liked to party and, of course, to spend time with that brown liquid friend of hers. My dad traveled for his work, so he was gone much of the time, and they never attended these leagues together until much later in their retirement years. Being in sheet metal work, dad would be called to jobs that lasted months in a factory somewhere out of state. He usually had an apartment in said city and would travel home every other weekend during any one stint. New Jersey was a frequent place of residence for him.

When I was about eleven years old, I heard my parents arguing about some lady named Lorraine. Apparently, dad sent checks bi-monthly to Lorraine, and mom suspected he might be supporting a child from an affair with her. Dad defended his actions as simply friendly support of a friend in financial need, but we all knew there was more to the story. We never brought it up so as not to hear what that "more" truly was. I have learned that it's pretty common for families to sweep away such secrets into the dust piles that hide quietly under the stove or fridge where nobody ever looks. How many people actually pull out the refrigerator to scrub the floor underneath?

And there was also that one time late into the night, I woke to my dad, leaning over the kitchen sink in the dark, talking on the phone very quietly while I crept on hands and knees down the hallway to listen. Undiscovered until my mom also overheard him and boldly picked up the other receiver, interrupting this clandestine tête-à-tête. I remember her brash retort in answer to what I later learned was the woman on the line asking her just what she was going to do about her *talking* to Norm, or about whatever else they did.

"What will I do, you ask?" In true Doris fashion, she came up with what she thought sounded threatening enough. "I'll claw your little eyes out. That's what!" My dad calmly chuckled, shaking his head as if this were not a very big deal. Doris shared this little story with friends many times in my presence, emphasizing her toughness in something like fighting for her man.

For reasons I do not fully understand, it almost always makes children sad when their parents do not want to stay together. And, of course, sometimes they mistakenly think they are at fault somehow. Knowing that I was unplanned and having one of those brothers who enjoyed teasing me-- saying that I was secretly adopted and everybody knew it but me, the responsibility of my parents' imminent divorce weighed heavily on my shoulders. As I grew older, I knew that alcoholism played somewhat of a role, and I presumed, by the little jibes my mom would make about my dad having a girlfriend on the side, that these were the real culprits of their marriage's demise. Little sips of poison seemingly taken from a slow-drip bottle hanging in our house infected the whole family and wore down the strength of their vows. But as children focus on the smaller picture with themselves as center stage, I could not help but think my intrusion into their lives had something to do with their unhappiness.

I can sift through my memories and find many moments full of laughter and fun—the freedom to run around our woods and play with the menagerie of animals welcomed in our home over the years. While I know I was determined at times to run away and maybe live in those woods by myself, circumstances always turned around and I felt safe at home. My parents did not hate each other. In fact, they lived like part-time roommates or siblings most of the time. There was no physical abuse and no knock-down-drag-out fights between Norm and Doris. Just a dark, weighty cloud that hung over them, and sometimes you could feel the dampness just walking in the room. Most of the time, Doris ignored this *weather* and went about her business, but once in a while, she would drum up a little fortitude and pronounce herself deserving of something better. In one of her moments of determination, mom decided that she would pack up and leave my dad, with me in tow, of course, since I was still quite young. My maternal grandparents lived in Florida, and mom thought their house would be a good escape. Now did she plan on actually living there, or was she just trying to send a message, I'm not sure. She bought us a couple of one-way plane tickets and packed only a few things to head south. We seemed to be exiting the house rather abruptly, as if my mom knew my dad might be on his way home. I recall her curt note, scrawled in pencil on a scrap piece of paper for my dad to find laying on the kitchen counter: "Michelle and I say

Goodbye." And off we went. Funny, I don't remember who drove us to the airport.

My dad got the message loud and clear and was appropriately contrite. That night in Florida, I overheard the hushed but cordial conversation between Norm and Doris where he made a quick plan to come down and get us, assuring her he wanted her to come home. My grandma chuckled and said that she never saw a couple so nice to each other while planning their divorce. Even my mom's lawyer, I heard her tell my grandmother, said they were too good of friends to get divorced.

And sure enough, they never did go through with the official breakup. I would relish the time, maybe years, thinking that all the affair business was in the past. And I never punished my dad for it. It just became a piece of knowledge that I could file in a dark green folder in the very back of the cabinet. I would keep placing new folders in the front of good memories and positive experiences that I might document with great photos to look back on later in life. Until the next time when we found ourselves getting wet from little drops that might fall from that dark cloud, and mom might threaten to leave again. I rode out many of these dips and twists on the proverbial roller coaster of my parents' relationship.

Mom remained in this marriage because it was easier than the effort it would take to go out on her own and make a comparable living, as she explained many times. My dad was "a good provider," according to Doris, and with him traveling much of the time, it was easy enough for her to stay and go about her own business. She had her life and he had his. Separate bowling and golf leagues on those Monday and Friday nights. Friends and bars and private lunch dates from her office as well, I suppose. While she justified her decision to stay, she did make sure to remind me often what a great sacrifice this was for her personally, knowing that my dad was the adulterer he was. "But I'm not going to scratch around to make a living when I can live here while he does his own thing and I do mine," she'd often say to justify her concession.

Part II

You who were regarded as distant from

Everyone but me

Remain so close

Spirits come and go like ghosts

11

Fitting the Puzzle Together

The prospect of one day meeting a half sibling or two was always in the back of my mind. Occasionally, I would search the white pages in New Jersey for the Giuseppe surname to see if I could find some unknown relatives, but then again, maybe my dad's illegitimate child, or children, would not have taken his name. I did not know the whole story and certainly never asked my dad. These things were best kept hidden, neatly set into boxes and stored out of sight in the dark corners of closets. But some nights, I'd crawl into that closet because it was fun to dream. I used to wonder if maybe a half brother or sister would look more like me than my own sister did, for she and I did not have one similar physical characteristic. Every time I asked why my sister chose to bleach her brilliant, chestnut hair to a bright blond while mine never darkened into that desired Italian hue, my dad would assure me that northern Italians often naturally grow lighter hair and have bluish, green eyes like mine. But my hair was also thin like my mother's while both siblings had thick, healthy locks. Why was I the only child who inherited that gene from my mom's side? I wondered if maybe a half sibling on dad's side might also look like a northern Italian.

My mom knew I knew the truth of my dad's infidelity and wondered how I could accept him and love him so unconditionally. I do not know the answer to that question either. I suppose I figured that his affair was something that just happened from weakness or loneliness at some point in his travels. And he then tried to make it right by this other woman with some sort of financial support. He never left us for this other family, so I gratefully noted that. I felt privileged that he was my dad, and I felt his pride every time he looked at me and called me his Half-pint or Sweet Pea.

As an adult, I know that's a rare gift to shore up self-worth and confidence. Somehow through many years of drunken Christmases and the overheard arguments between my parents, I grew into a fairly stable, emotionally healthy adult. In my more recent years, I have heard all the Christian psychology—girls need their fathers to place a very specific puzzle piece. If that father is missing, that space will, like a magnet, constantly draw misshapen pieces, and she will try to force them to fit, even if it means cutting a new shape of that hole. My dad gently put that puzzle together right for me a long time ago.

My sister, of course, missed my dad after his death too, but maybe, I thought at the time, not the same way I did. She asked me once while we sat in lawn chairs by her pool,

"Do you really have all that many memories of him? I only have a few. He was gone so much. I mean, yeah, he came to my softball games and we went on fishing trips, for sure. He was a good dad, but I can't remember him around a whole lot of my childhood or teenage years."

"I do. Yes. But then again, I have a different way of storing my childhood memories."

The question fell out long before I had any suspicion of my dad not being glued to my DNA, so my smile as I answered my sister was one of peace. Peace that he was mine. Peace that he loved me unconditionally. Peace that even death could not change that love and somehow negate it.

"I remember the smell of dad—his after shave mixed with a little cigar smoke that settled in his clothes, and a touch of woodsy air that always followed him from the great outdoors. I remember his little chuckle that came from deep within and brought up with it that ever-present, sleepy phlegm that rested in his chest. I remember looking into his eyes, almost like they were mirrors—like I could see myself the way he saw me—valuable.

He obviously valued my sister too, fiercely. He had this hard shell around himself that made him seem callus at times, like when he would call the boys always chasing after Toni *bulls*.

"I don't want those bulls hanging around here when I'm not home. Maybe I need them to see me polishing my guns as warning, eh?"

We had plenty of deer heads, moose horns and pheasants adorning our basement walls, the only place in the house my mom allowed such décor. My dad must have kept the local taxidermist in business, a faithful customer. Our young friends surely feared the wild boar with the curly white fangs protruding out the sides. They told of nightmares about that beast. But the piece everyone was drawn to the most was the velvety, black bear skin hanging on the wall.

Many times, I would stand against it and let the fur engulf me like a cave girl's warm winter coat. I never could get the true story of where my dad caught that big bear since every time I asked him to tell me, he'd sincerely claim that it was chasing my sister down the street and he simply had to save her. *Down the streets of Detroit?* He'd shake his head in earnest.

"Yes, right down this street here. You wouldn't want me to let it live and take your sister for its dinner, now, would you?"

Evenings at our house were dark as mom and dad's habit was to drink in front of the television well past sunset. Soon dad would be asleep in his lounger and mom would be nodding off with a spacey look, not often all that attentive to the program on at the time. Pulling the car up the driveway after dark used to elicit some drag in my stomach as the eerie, fluorescent green glow of the TV shone through the front picture window even though the curtains were drawn, neither one of them motivated enough to get up and turn on a little lamp. Advice from eye doctors who suggested you light the darkness, they just labeled as psychobabble. Always watched TV in shadows, and a slight tension radiated off the two of them. On the inside, it could feel creepy during the right kind of show.

One time in this familiar soupy atmosphere, my dad's low snore under the volume of the television, my sister's car sounded in the driveway. As she walked to the front door across the lawn, something startled her, and she let out a scream. It could have sounded like background noise, but it woke my dad in an instant, and until that point, I had never seen him move so fast. Up from a prone position. Off the lounger and out the front door before I even registered the sound. What would he have done to an attacker? He was no young, fit, muscular father. But his instinct, nevertheless, was to protect her. Dad had no fear—he was the kind of father we girls dream about as we long for security. One that will enter the most dangerous situations and rescue us if we need rescuing.

I remember my own daughter after watching the movie, *Taken*, asking her dad if she ever got kidnapped, would he come find her like Liam Neeson did, hoping for affirmation that he could. I think it is inborn in us to want to trust in such protection. Turns out, in the case of my sister that night, it was just a friend waiting out there for her to get home. Profuse apologies to my dad followed. Dad just shook his head and, with a little chuckle, muttered something about "these bulls nowadays."

12

A Crumbling Foundation

When my mom finally told me her own secret, I received the news with a calm that surprised us both. We sat in my small living room with the Christmas tree still up in January, sort of relaxing until mom displayed some unintentional shakes of her right leg as she scooted to the edge of the couch to express something important. She started with the claim that she was not a good mother.

"I'm so very sorry I let you down and was so terrible to you. It's overwhelming now."

But I did not hold this judgement of her, and I assured her that her sins, so-to-speak, do not define fully a good or bad mother.

"Mom, you did the best you could. I turned out fine, and I am happy now."

I thought at first that she was referring to her alcoholism. We had already come to terms with that flaw and had overcome any issues I felt about it during childhood. I had even read the Al-Anon literature and philosophies and had those twelve steps shelved somewhere in my head by now. Why would she choose this point to admit that *this* shortcoming made her an overall poor mother? I didn't think she was so bad, and I had worked out the meaning of forgiveness, or at least acceptance, by this point anyway, never wanting her to suffer for any of her past offenses.

"But you don't know all of it," she continued. "I had . . . a relationship throughout your childhood that I never told

you about, and that's surely not what a *good* mother does."
She gazed downward and couldn't look me in the eye.

I braced myself then. Okay—stop. Think. A *relationship?*
When? Really, when did she have time for this? How could I
have never known or seen signs of such a relationship? She
has never been able to keep any other secret tied up and
muffled so securely.

"Okay," I said, drawing out the pause. "Okay. I can
understand how that could happen, you know, with dad
being gone so much. Plus, even more so, you had to live with
the knowledge that he had had a girlfriend for many years." I
really could not be angry with her for this admission. Really,
who am I to judge?

"I don't think you can ever forgive me for this. It is so
wrong." Tears crawled down her cheeks, and she covered her
face with her hands, a gesture of regret or repentance that I
never remembered seeing her do before.

Truthfully, the part of it that I kept thinking was "wrong"
was that my mom had always vilified my dad for having an
affair. If she were just as guilty, why did she always make him
out to be the only bad guy?

"We had an ongoing relationship. . . for fifteen years." She
said that last part rather quietly.

Fifteen? Fifteen. Until I was a teenager, I assumed,
depending on when it started. I wasn't thinking clearly
enough to ask exactly when it began and when it ended.

Apparently, my mom thought that her recent diagnosis of
cirrhosis of the liver would take her life soon, for doctors had
not given her very long to live with a liver that was pretty
much shot by the time they detected her disease. And she

finally had to get this off her chest before her time came. You know, confess and make amends and all that twelve-step stuff.

The news shifted my world to such an extent that I struggled to find footing. Knowing one truth—the truth of my dad's guilty life sentence—and finding out that another truth coexisted was difficult to grasp. My mother had never even hinted at her own guilt while I was growing up. She guarded this truth with an acumen I never knew she possessed. She was never mysteriously missing from my childhood days or nights. She never travelled with friends; in fact, I was always with her on any trips she did take without the rest of our family, her little traveling companion, since I was so far in years from the other kids. This was not simply a one-time affair that she kept hidden but a whole separate life she managed to conceal. How could this have gone on for fifteen years, many of those years right under my nose? And I was a pretty perceptive kid, so things didn't easily slip by me.

For the first year or so of *knowing*, I had to take her at her word. This other man was not my biological father. Wouldn't I have met him at some point or another if he were? He would have seen her throughout her pregnancy with me. Wouldn't he have questioned? Wouldn't her tell, that flaw that showed up any other time she had something juicy to hide, have given her secret away? She assured me they had used birth control every single time they were together, whereas with my father, she never used protection, as, of course, they didn't need to. I think I asked his name, but I do not remember if she answered me or not. My dad was my dad no matter what, and I told myself it would not even matter if he were not biological. I loved him fiercely, and I knew he loved me. My mom and I never spoke of her affair again, especially since we had to deal with the extreme effects of her disease in the years to come.

But as years passed after my mom eventually succumbed to cirrhosis, I began to unwittingly allow the fear that maybe my dad was not my *real* dad slink into my psyche. What does fear feel like? When it first visits, it feels like a foggy cloud that seeps into your brain and makes you strain your eyes to see anything else through it. As it lingers, fear becomes lead filler in your stomach or a heavy weight upon your shoulders. If you could touch it, it would feel cold and strong, like steel. Fear even has a smell. It is the pungency that causes the gag reflex—the pit in your stomach to rise and demand to be expelled. Only it's too big to come out. It can remain for years, a parasite infecting the rest of your system, as it did mine.

I began having stomach issues, strange nausea, and motion sickness. I began having difficulty talking about my Italian heritage, especially with my cousins who loved to discuss delectable, Italian food and travel to our ancestors' hometowns in northern Italy. I found excuses not to go to our annual family reunions in West Virginia. I couldn't get myself to go and maybe meet even more distant cousins on my dad's side and wonder if we really were related or not.

Many people, or maybe most, live happily with a stepparent or an adoptive parent. They bond appropriately whether they are genetically related or not. The love seeps right into the bloodstream and overpowers those genetic

78

threads. Most adoptees rest at peace with their parental affiliations, nurture being more important than nature, as long as the nurture was appropriate. But I was no longer at peace. This was no adoption. This was a profound deception. If it were true that I was not my dad's progeny, my whole perception of who I *was* would shatter catastrophically. As was already happening at this point, something in me was crumbling piece by piece like an old faulty cement foundation does. It would be like waking up one day and no longer being the person you were the day before.

13
An Angry Storm Brewing

Norm was brave. I always thought I inherited this trait with only a few exceptions. I was never afraid to speak my mind, or even to speak formally in front of a group, one of the most common fears people claim. As an educator, I certainly practiced the skill quite often. I attempted any sport and found enough coordination to build my confidence, though I never did join a team. I set out with a friend once to swim all the way across a lake with no planning or anticipation of tiring out.

Leeches, on the other hand, were a thing of nightmares. The vision of twenty, or maybe a hundred and twenty, of them attached to my sister's legs haunted me in childhood. Dad told me that leeches would melt right off a person if you salted them, so I snuck the kitchen saltshaker into my beach bag every time we went canoeing on the Huron River, for I certainly would never give up canoeing any chance I got just because leeches teemed in those waters when I had a weapon.

A scar marks the bottom of my chin from a slide headfirst down Suicide Peak, a steep sledding hill in the way-back of our woods, about a half mile or so from our house, by Eliza Howell Park. While a teenaged boy climbed up the hill towing his wooden toboggan behind, I waited at the top, looking over the edge for my lane like a responsible little girl of seven years old, but a thoughtless other neighbor boy pushed my sled down before I was ready. Speeding down that icy hill, neither one of us could have avoided what was about to happen. My face and the corner of the boy's toboggan met in a head-on collision even as he tried to swing it out of the way.

Spotted black dots danced in front of my eyes. Then a yellow filter seemed to alter the whole landscape. Finally, I saw the red drops under me as someone lifted me up to the top of the hill to get to the trail and walk all the way home.

Guilt-ridden Toboggan Boy, who unnecessarily felt responsible, half carried me along the snowy path as my legs seemed to melt and refused to support me. The boy who actually was responsible for the accident was nowhere-to-be-found. Toboggan Boy held a scarf to my chin to stave off the blood, and when we got home, my mom threw me in the car, grabbed her purse and took me to the hospital. She told my dad later that "meat was hanging down from the gash."

The side of my face swelled to the size of a cantaloupe, and apparently some intern must have sewed me up because the scar was jagged and rough. Surely, they must have advised plastic surgery for a later date, but the way my dad always phrased it sounded a little scary: "We need to take you in to get that recut." For years afterward, looking at me, my dad would stop mid-conversation, run his thumb over the marred skin and utter those words, but I was game for it. I bolstered up the courage: "Let's go. Let's get it recut." But we never did. I wore the scar like it built character. I was not the only child left with wounds from Suicide Peak. Mary from across the street still wears what looks like a long centipede etched around her knee from grazing a tree stump on the way down. My friends and I often played the game of naming what near catastrophe caused this or that heroic mark. Many people in my life today say they do not notice that scar on my face at all. It's funny because when I look in the mirror, sometimes it's all I see. The scar seems to be getting deeper, cutting a prominent groove, mimicking those internal scars we procure as we make our way through life's tangled paths. And when sifting through a treasure box of memories, yanking out and reexamining family stories the way you would old heirlooms and laying them out before me with a new perspective, I run my fingers over many jagged marks. Should I recut them now?

Later, as a 17-year-old, I drove hours through a blizzard in Canada at night when I could not see anything but the tiny red taillights from the car in front of me. Sure, I gripped the steering wheel tightly, but I was confident that I would eventually make it home. I had the tenacity, or dare I say, stubbornness of a typical Italian woman raised in a family with such dynamics as one might assume the Giuseppes possessed.

Now that I look back and really think about the memory of swimming across that lake, the truth that surfaces and waves its hand in front of my face to get my attention is saying, "You did not actually make it all the way." My friend Krissy and I stopped about halfway to the other shoreline and rethought our endeavor. As we treaded water, we discussed the very sure task ahead—we could continue swimming and make it to the banks on the other side. We had come this far. It was not so insurmountable to continue that same distance the rest of the way. We were not even that tired yet. At least not completely exhausted. And then we could say we truly did it. But there wasn't much over there to see—just bushes and rocks going up to who-knows-where on land. And we remembered that giant pike, preserved and mounted on the wall back at the cabin sporting some pretty sharp teeth. Somebody caught that fish in this very lake, so others like it could be swimming underneath us at this moment. If we continued onward, we would then still have to swim all the way back. We could, instead, turn around now and swim back to our shore, knowing that we had it in us to swim the whole way across if we really wanted to. Should we tell people we swam the whole distance without explaining the technicality of turning around mid-swim? I think we ended up believing our own justification of the story—that we did, indeed, swim the lake across. Turning around was not, after all, all that brave, but we built it up in our minds that halfway there and back was the same distance anyway as swimming all the way across. My confidence was strong like my dad's, but how it panned out in reality was, admittedly, something else.

Day trips out to the lakes were frequent in our family. Packing a cooler with sausages to grill and drinks to keep cold was a habit we adopted long ago. While I was content with cans of Lipton sweet, iced tea or Dr. Pepper, Doris and Norm packed plenty of whisky and Diet 7-Up.

On one occasion after the heat of the day tired us all out and we were sprawled on various lawn chairs, a fierce storm awoke and poised to break loose. The clouds grew darker with each passing moment. This was before the age of smart phones, but we did not need the weather app to tell us what was coming. Yellow and green mixed with dark grey meant that this could be tornadic. An eerie calm confirmed the warning. There was a sheltered pavilion under which we all began stacking our supplies to wait it out. Dad wanted to leave, though, and get home before the storm fully unleashed. He appeared to be packing up to head to the car. For two reasons, this was not wise.

"What do you think you're doing" my mom asked rhetorically. "We are not leaving in this weather. And you've had too much to drink anyway." Her hands on her hips for emphasis. "Honestly, he thinks he can do anything," she said in our direction with an exaggerated eye roll.

"Eh, you have plenty of rides here," he retorted. "You can get home whenever you want. I'm leaving."

"Please, it's too dangerous. Just wait a little while. Look at that sky."

And with that, he ignored her protests and looked in my direction with a wink. He was not worried in the least, and he drove off despite the ugly colors on the horizon, almost shaking his fist at them, daring them to cross him.

I stood under that pavilion as droplets of water began shooting down like little bullets onto our recently vacated picnic tables and watched his perfectly-sunny-sky-blue Buick trail off down the lake shore drive, rain getting heavier by the second. While the storm clouds had gathered forces, the wind stood at bay. Almost backing down just for him. They blew a little steam in an attempt to intimidate but quickly resigned themselves to the fact that they were not going to win. What's a little water to contend with? I turned back toward the others and shrugged, somehow with no real doubt that he would make it home. And he did. *His* confidence always did pan out. After a short wait under shelter, the rain turned docile like a sleepy kitten after some rough play, curling up for a rest.

14

Pretending We are Twins

Leaving the Detroit Public Schools in seventh grade for a small private school in the neighborhood across the freeway brought me in contact with many Polish Catholic families. Several students surely had familiar Italian roots, and a few Irish or a Scott sat along the sidelines too. But most of my middle school classmates had the common 'ski at the ends of their surnames. I didn't want to be Polish…and it was not because of the silly Polish jokes we threw at each other in fun. In fact, Italian insults were popular too; being called a dago or a wop never bothered me because I didn't know they were derogatory labels at the time, for dad often affectionately called himself a wop with his familiar, wet laugh accompanying the joke. The Italian characteristics I found here at my new school felt warm as they circled around me and made me smile.

Later in life, a friend's mom, an immigrant from Italy, told me she always treasured a name from the old country and desired to christen her firstborn son, Diego, but it was too close to the slur, so she saved him from the ridicule he would undoubtedly incur and named him Enzo instead.

All of us kids bounced what are now considered insensitive phrases against each other on the playground and later laughed together all through school with no real offense ever sticking. But we were sure clear on what ethnicity each one claimed with pride.

Still, I preferred to align more fully or, what we now might say, identify with the fewer Italians rather than with the ethnic group in the majority at St. Gemma. One particular companion and I became fast friends because we looked much like sisters. Mary Jane had a stronger, more athletic build but the same dirty blond, shaggy, fine hair, and eastern European facial features—prominent cheekbones and lack of definition to our little mouths. Mary Jane's mother made the best sandwiches for her sack lunches, and she was generous enough to trade me half of hers for half of my more traditional peanut butter and jellies most days. I even threw in my Chips Ahoy cookie as extra bargaining, for I savored that thin-sliced, Polish deli meat with a little lettuce and tomato stacked between artisan bread slices—much better than the *Wonder Bread* we carried at our house. She and I began to run together, study together, and, eventually, choose the same private high school to attend after eighth grade.

At our new high school, teachers oftentimes confused the two of us if we happened to be separated in the hallways or in specific classes. I was called Mary Jane so many times, I stopped correcting these mistakes. Other students sometimes asked us if we were twins, while most did not even bother to ask. The assumption was understandable, especially since they saw us arrive together daily as we carpooled from Detroit. Mary Jane and I let the assumption fly and just began telling people it was true that we were, in fact, sisters.

Only my childhood friend of Italian descent, the other Mary across the street, did not seem to care for this little game we played. I think she wanted me to own my Italian ethnicity so we could keep that affinity between just the two of us. She would never acknowledge that Mary Jane and I looked alike at all. She often reminded me that she could not see what everyone was talking about.

"You are Italian, Michelle. Mary Jane is not—you don't look the same at all. You have the darker, more olive skin tone. And in some lights, your eyes look pure green, just like your dad's. You and your brother look exactly alike, and you see how dark and Italian he is. How could you think you look Polish?"

"I'm just going by what everyone else says," I would argue with a shrug of my shoulders.

"I mean strangers at church or every new teacher at school always asks us. If you could just see how they struggle with choosing the right name when they see one of us at a time in the hallway. They simply guess Mary Jane or Michelle and hope they get the right one."

My mom was not snarky or even offended about it, but she never admitted that we looked alike either. Mary Jane and I are still friends today. She keeps her hair much blonder than mine these days, and we don't travel in all the same circles anymore, so the game of pretending we are twins is nothing but a fond memory.

Unless I start to think about it in light of my mom's secret, that is.

15
The House My Grandfather Built

I finally did go to one of the Italian family reunions with my favorite cousins and my sister, perhaps to search for more signs. I was feeling particularly secure at this time—relatives were feeling extra close as the older generation present told stories of the past. Fond memories passed around like a fresh pitcher of lemonade shared among friends.

Flipping through a booklet of descendants that one of my cousins compiled, I stopped and fingered a picture of my great-great grandfather. He sported a curly-cue, white mustache with hints of black left from his youth. And he had my father's eyes. I leaned in and searched those eyes, looking for myself. I studied the shape of his mouth, his nose, his ears. I could see my grandpa, and I could see my dad. But, of course, I could not see myself at all. This did not mean much because how was I, a woman, to see myself in a male relative from the 1800s anyway? I continued flipping page by page through the years and studying photographs of grandchildren and great grandchildren. Myself included. My name was written into the family tree just as if it belonged there. In permanent ink. Child of Norm and Doris Giuseppe.

On this trip, my cousin and that same 85-year-old aunt Celia walked with me down the street of the small town of Thomas to see the house in which she and my dad grew up; the house that their father built with his own two hands. I remember many visits to my grandfather's other house in

Detroit. His workshop had a distinct smell of sawdust and wood. As a child, I was fascinated with the seemingly old-fashioned tools he used. And I was lucky he let me try my hand at some of them once in a while. My favorite activity was to sit at the grinding wheel, pedaling furiously, as hard as I could, to see how fast I could make it spin. You would resist the urge to touch it lest you wanted to burn off a layer of skin. He was a talented artist. I saved a bookshelf he made before my birth and still use it today, enjoying the chance to tell my own grandchildren that it has been passed down from their great, great grandfather.

The idea of this little walk was to catch a glimpse of this house in Thomas, West Virginia and perhaps sneak into the backyard to look around and imagine my dad and his siblings running up and down the hills and crags of this property. As we rounded the back door, a young couple peeked out of the screened window.

"Can I help you," the man asked. I explained that my grandfather had built this house and my dad, and my aunt standing right here with me now, grew up here, so we were just looking around curiously.

"Didn't mean to bother anyone," I said sheepishly. Immediately, the man knew the family name.

"You must be here for that reunion. We still call this house 'the Giuseppe House.' Would you like to come in and look around? We would be happy to let you all reminisce."

This was more than we could have dreamed. Yes, we wanted to come in. My aunt's feebleness disappeared as she breathed in energy and stood a little taller, as if drawn up with a string. Her excitement kept expressing itself in little squeals that would escape before she had the chance to stifle them in present company.

The owners of this house, both current and past through a hundred years, preserved the original woodworking and design. It was surreal to walk through a house that looked just as it did when my dad and his sister lived here. My grandfather carved these banisters and built those recessed cabinets with knotty pine and maple. I ran my hands over the railing as we walked up the stairs—over the very exposed wood that my dad walked upon in a different time. My aunt must have been feeling such a strange sense of nostalgia. She became quiet and contemplative, except for the moments of happy recounts of how my dad jumped out of this window or hid things in that cubby. We even climbed up into the attic that still showed old, peeling wallpaper scraps on one wall from the time my aunt played dolls up there in the 1930s. I could smell that familiar wood that brought me back to my childhood. Back to my grandfather's workshop. Back to my dad. The connection was so vivid that I knew I simply could not experience such a visceral sense if my dad were not living in my bloodstream.

I decided to embrace this reality and get more involved in the reunion's activities. I conversed with some relatives I had previously kept behind the imaginary screen I had erected between us. I laughed at the old 8-millimeter films someone had converted for this event, remembering how many times my dad had showed us these movies and had had to splice back together sections of the soundless film.

I exchanged Linkedin contacts with distant cousins I had never met before. I listened and danced to the old Italians, who happened to be great uncles, playing the accordion and banjo at the town tavern, called *The Purple Cow.*

A group of us reverently visited the old cemetery and sought out the grave of one of the old progenitors of our family. We paid our respects to those early founders buried here, down to our own grandparents who passed within months of each other. In 1983, we had followed a special hearse along those country roads carrying each of their bodies to settle them into this cemetery. West Virginia. As the country song goes, "almost heaven," where they could rest among their ancestors. "Home."

16

Sweet Pea

The experience of exploring this house was one of the best in my life. One that teased me with assurance for a while. It resurrected memories of my grandparents making ravioli in our tiny kitchen in Detroit on the metal grey and white flecked Formica table. Sweat dripping down the sides of Grandma's temple and pooling around the back of her collar, making her hair frizz a little. Sheets of pasta draped over little drying racks, makeshift from old wooded dowels set over glasses and dishes. Forming the gnocchi by rolling a grape-sized piece of dough between the palm of her hand and a metal grater—into what we called rats because the dumplings resembled the little baby rodents. Mom loved telling friends we were having rats for dinner and then watching them all react in horror.

My dad was the cook—he would simmer his red sauce with pork or beef short ribs, infusing the pasta sauce with a hearty flavor I have only tasted once since his death at an authentically Italian restaurant in Dearborn. I cried unexpectantly—could not contain my tears upon the first bite of familiar sauce all those years after his death. The aroma of fresh tomatoes, sizzling gamey meat, oil and garlic is home.

While my dad lay recovering in the rehabilitation center, he lamented not fully teaching me that family recipe. I had watched him but was too young to care how to do it back then, and we had planned on having a lesson as an adult now that I had a family of my own to feed. His brush with death came so suddenly that he was caught still planning for the future when he was brought down by the infected appendix's poison attacking his weak heart. Walking around that old house in Thomas, I inhaled the imaginary smell of the red sauce still bubbling on the stove.

People in my life like to ask about my Italian heritage, especially when talking food. Well into adulthood, it started showing up that I did inherit my dad's fondness for cooking. And the method of seasoning or creating. I guess it is the aversion to following actual written recipes that is common to most Italians. We just make it up as we go along. The usual, "a little bit of this and a little bit of that." Colleagues assume I will know the best place to find an authentic Italian meal, and they also know they better not ever suggest the answer is Olive Garden.

"You're Italian, Michelle, what the heck do I do with eggplant? I've tasted eggplant parmesan before but have no idea how to get this vegetable to act something like lasagna noodles, let alone how to make it taste good." And there I am again in the school cafeteria at the high school where I work telling the group of teachers how to make a good lasagna to impress their friends at a dinner party.

"First of all, noodles from scratch is always the way to go, though I don't make them myself. It's easy to purchase them from the Italian market, and you might even get to talk to the Nonna as she's sending that dough through the press. And then using a fresh tomato sauce is a necessity. Don't add dried oregano just because you see that ingredient in the blend of

'Italian' spices. Few, fresh ingredients work together for the best taste."

My dad once rated my style of cooking and gathering food in comparison to his mother's back in her time. He said I was not quite living like they did in the '30s and '40s where he and his brother or his best friend Benny, who couldn't read or write a lick, would hunt those forests in West Virginia in their worn-out overalls, baggy and soiled like the illustrations of Huck Finn fishing along the banks of the Mississippi. They'd dump their dead rabbits and pheasants on the porch for their mom to pick up, skin and simmer for dinner. I could never manage something like that. It wasn't the norm for my time.

But I also didn't seem quite a member of my own generation either.

I took his rating as a great compliment, and he meant it that way too. I would not use packaged meals or buy meat already processed and wrapped in plastic. I frequented the local butcher and farm markets when my children were little to make them the most natural food I could find—wanting to teach them preparation skills that were becoming obsolete for many in that same generation. I wanted them to associate the smell of sauce boiling or freshly cut cucumbers with home the way I did.

No wonder my dad chose the little piece of heaven just situated on the outskirts of the city to plant his roots in Michigan, keeping the familiarity of the hills he came from close to his chest. Even on a tiny plot of land in Detroit, my dad fit in his tomato and zucchini plants. It was my job to water them, and while spraying water from the hose on the plants, the fragrance became potent, wafting up and encircling me with comfort.

My dad and I would eat those tomatoes off the vine as if they were apples, sprinkling a tiny bit of salt before each bite. He grew peas along the side fence in the backyard and would hand me a basket. "Go pick those pea pods, Sweet Pea. We'll have them with dinner tonight." I can eat those little green pearls like candy today.

17

Coffee Percolating

My parents never had a schedule for us kids like some parents I have come to observe today. We went to bed when we wanted and slept in however late we felt motivated to do...or unmotivated. My sister, especially, being a teenager when I was still so young and impressionable, often slept in till noon. Memories of her out with her friends until late into the night play around in the back of my mind. I might wake up some nights as she would keep trying that pesky key that would not slide into its hole obediently, attempting a quiet entry but alerting our mother anyway, and Doris never could whisper.

"Where the hell have you been," she'd exclaim, just as an acknowledgement that she noticed, never really expecting an answer. Dad never said a word, on the rare occasions he was home, that is; some estimate of his time home hovers around a couple weekends a month is all. Not sure if that is accurate or not. I also adopted the habit of sleeping in late on the days I didn't have school, but on those mornings with dad present, I would wake in the morning to the tantalizing aroma and purr of percolating coffee. Even if it was a cheap brand like *Maxwell House*, all coffee smells good when percolated rather than hastily run through today's automatic drip machines, producing dirty water that appears in such a hurry to cool down, forcing multiple thirty-second zaps in the microwave, a convenience that did not exist in our home, for my dad thought the waves were dangerous and would not dream of cooking what were called "TV dinners" back then. Bad enough that the next generation ate McDonalds for dinner. We never did. No family of his would eat some frozen meal wrapped in plastic.

The smell would lure me out of bed to find my dad standing over the stove with a cast iron skillet set on the big burner, heating oil to fry his freshly grated potatoes piled high like a pale haystack next to the pan. I would sit on the leather-like-plastic kitchen chair and watch. Dad might say, "Good Morning, Sunshine. Ready for some breakfast?" I would always talk him into making waffles on that black, plug-in waffle iron that was so hard to clean afterwards. Eggs, potatoes, sausage, waffles, real butter . . .and juice for me. I loved the smell of the coffee and the delightful dance of the golden-brown bubbles reaching all the way to the top of that clear glass percolator cap, but I could not stomach the liquid back then. Sometimes my dad would sneak a shot of Tia Maria into his cup and let me try a sip. It was a fun little secret, but I never got on board. Even as an adult.

Mom and dad bought me a coffee maker for Christmas at least three times in my early married years. I always returned it and tried to tell them we had no use for it at our house, not realizing, in my immaturity, that the gift may not have been for me. I am sure it annoyed them that when they came over for a holiday meal, or when they stayed over on visits to our place down in Florida where we lived for a couple years, we had no coffee to offer. Mom and dad would drive to a Dunkin Donut shop and bring their coffee back in paper cups with a lid, as if they could not survive without it. Hence the several gifts trying to convert us to proper social conventions.

It was not until dad lay in that intensive care hospital bed for weeks on end that I graduated from smelling coffee to drinking it. At our bedside vigils, kind nurses would bring in a cup of comfort—even to hold onto like a warm pair of fuzzy mittens. My routine for those couple of months was to drop my kids off at school in the morning and go sit with my dad for a couple of hours, quietly praying or trying to talk him into fighting this attack on his body. We had frequent family meetings down the hall in a room with my mom, my brother and the team of doctors working on his case. Their town's local pastor, an angel who became our genuine friend, visited daily. Walking those halls, talking with our crew, sitting with my dad, always involved coffee. We had free run of the little family lounge with a cappuccino machine, dosing surprisingly flavorful espresso, at our service, so, of course, we offered a warm beverage to every visitor, like normal people do. And drinking together became a special companionship. Something you did with allies all rooting for Norm's recovery.

Even though my dad recovered, in a way, he was never able to come home to enjoy good health again. We did drink coffee together, though, at the rehab center in Ann Arbor. If only he knew how *won over* I actually am these days. How annoyed, or maybe appalled, I am when someone does not offer coffee in their home. How I created a "coffee station" featuring various flavors and add-ins for each visitor's tastes, though dad would drink it black. How we all have a favorite cup that helps bring out the best experience with our morning cuppa. How many coffee makers we have gone through now to get the perfect taste. My favorite is a miniature espresso, stove-top percolator that hisses before it's done, shooting the aroma throughout the kitchen and down the hall, flirting with anyone nearby. I usually think of dad as I sip my coffee, and oftentimes, I make waffles on the iron he gave me for Christmas one year. The iron looks brand new twenty-five years later. *That* gift I never returned.

18

Queen Anne's Lace

With my sister coming to Detroit for a visit, I cleaned my house and readied the spare bedroom with freshly cleaned sheets and a mist of linen spray called "Meadows and Fields." That reminded me to gather some real wild flowers for her room in homage to our days playing in the woods. Arranging some sprigs of Queen Anne's Lace in a hobnail, milk glass vase drew my eye to the single tiny, dark speck in the middle of the flower cluster. That little purple flower in the middle is hardly noticeable unless you know to look for it. I had examined Queen Anne's Lace many times in wonderment of that design. When you see a field of the flowers, you just see what looks like bolts of fabric and white lace. But when you go closer and study the anatomy of the flower, you see more detail, but that detail remains hidden from those who never really care go close enough. Most are happy to metaphorically drive by fields of life and appreciate the cottony white, ignoring the tiny contrast sitting right there--dead center, staring them in the face.

During some unusual private time with my sister, I began to ask some questions.

"So Sis, tell me. Did you and mom ever talk about her love life? I've learned something about her that I find really hard to believe. Especially since I never heard about this before, and you know how mom couldn't keep a secret to save her life. Maybe you already knew about her 'relationship'?" Turns out Antoinette did know of my mom's affair in real time. She even met the man once or twice.

"Of course I knew mom had a boyfriend. How could you not? I'm sure. I thought we all knew that." She forgets that I am much younger than her so, as a child, I would have been unaware of the obvious, I guess. And my sister inherited the secret-keeping gene as well, at least for this secret anyway. Hers was not a healthy view of men, and so she harbored no guilt about hiding things from them. She sometimes hung in the same establishments with her older friends drinking with my mom's cronies. My questions aroused some worried suspicion in her as well, but that misgiving seemed directed at me.

"Why are you even questioning this? You can't possibly imagine that mom's boyfriend had anything to do with you? You were already ten years old when I met him anyway." What my sister may not have known was that my mom admitted to me that this *affair* was really a fifteen-year relationship. No assurance could come of the fact that I was already running around the block and riding bikes by the time my sister met the man. *When* exactly this relationship began was the real question.

"What was this man like? Was he nice? Did you like him? Do you remember his name?"

Do I look like him? I wanted to ask that last question but could not quite get it out.

It never occurred to Antoinette to question where I came from or that it could be anything other than what she grew up believing. She also claims to know just when my conception happened—on a whole-family Canadian vacation where mom turned up pregnant soon after. The problem is, that story is not flush with the one my aunt shared previously. The one that sounded quite certain that my mom and dad were alone on a trip driving down to Florida. These stories are as far away from each other as north and south, in fact. Aunt Celia's story also made me curious. Where were the other two kids at the time of their trip? Who was staying with them, and why were my parents headed down south alone?

All Antoinette remembers about this boyfriend is that he too was married at the time and had quite a few children. And his surname was something that sounded Polish, maybe ending with 'ski.

"Just don't worry about it now," her assurance a little forced. "It doesn't even matter. Who cares? Even if he were your 'sperm donor,'" exaggerated air quotes added, "we are still family no matter what. You are my sister either way. No one ever has to know any different. And besides, look at you—you got the nice, strong teeth, unlike the rest of us. And maybe you didn't get that alcoholism gene either." A chuckle escapes. "No, all kidding aside, you look just like dad anyway. There's no question." We seemed to gather up this conversation like a stack of notes. Tap, tap, tap. All corners even. Bound together. And now we have put it away, or even discarded it as trash.

Of course, I wondered if she knew more than she was revealing. My friend, Suspicion, or my nemesis, and I had become quite close by this point.

DNA testing gained popularity in the years surrounding my family reunion trip. While that trip renewed some hope in me that I felt a connection with these relatives due to a genetic sort of resonance, a desire to confirm that truth brewed beneath the surface of my confidence. My sister had tried to quash those thoughts with the assertion that we could never really know for sure since both my dad and the man in question were no longer with us—as if we needed them present to do a good old fashioned paternity test. This was shortly before the many stories of people finding out one parent or another was not biological started cropping up on the internet or in documentaries. I could surely do the DNA testing to see what my roots were. I could look for that Italian heritage that could only show up in me from the Giuseppe lineage, for my mom's ancestors came from other parts of Europe.

Stomach bugs became more frequent for me in my late 40s. It seemed I was sensitive to all kinds of common foods that others eat regularly. Traveling, something I had always enjoyed, became a challenge as I never knew how I would feel being trapped in a car or on a plane with the nausea and sharp pains doubling me over at times and not knowing just what food to avoid to prevent these sudden attacks. After one bout of what I assumed was food poisoning, I lay in bed experiencing the lack of energy that always followed. Legs and arms felt weighted down. With my mouth full of paste holding it closed and my eyes striving to focus, I sat up in bed. The urgency of grabbing a pail in which to vomit had passed, and I needed to get up and get myself some water.

Stepping onto the floor tested my sanity, or at least my wakefulness. Was this seriously real? I felt as if I were back standing on our little fishing boat we used to take out on the lake. We liked to test our balance and coordination by trying to walk the boat while someone else tipped it back and forth with their legs. I can still hear my brother's taunting laughter as he would strive a little too hard to make me topple over the edge of the boat.

I lifted my knees up way too high trying to get a footing. But the boat-like floor tilted and slanted to the right and then to the left. The room rocked. My arms stretched out before me reached toward the doorway, and my shoulder slammed into the wall. A brief, unexpected chuckle escaped as I gripped the door jamb, rubbing what would later be a bruised shoulder.

I had heard of vertigo but never experienced it before. Dehydration must have brought on drastic changes within the delicate neurochemistry of my brain. It was kind of funny to think that the human brain could fool you like this. The movement of the room felt real. I was surely awake and sane in every other way. I could reason with myself that this was a result of my sickness and not actually my house floating on a body of water, but the reality was that I lost all stability for those moments. Vertigo threw me into the wall and shook me to the point where I could not stand steadily. I could not will it to stop. It was my reality. And I waited, holding on, hoping that the bubble would creep back to the middle of the level.

Vertigo has no real cure. Just tricks and techniques, like the Epley maneuver to try to remedy the life-altering symptoms. Some people have had luck with antihistamines, but people who do not find relief can go crazy. The dizziness and shifting ground can stop you in your tracks. I've known people stuck in an occurrence who really can't go anywhere for fear of moving too much and feeling themselves pulled into that swirling whirlpool.

It's like that with life sometimes. You walk around on sure, solid ground moving forward in a direction you chose for your life, and then an episode of vertigo takes you down and changes everything.

19

The Floor Drops

The fear parasite spawned in adulthood kept me from actually purchasing a DNA testing kit for a while. Part of me wanted to confirm my Italian bloodline and finally extinguish this enemy called Doubt with a capital D in bold print. Doubt had grown so strong in recent years that I could visualize the rejoicing and freedom I could experience should I kill this villain with sound evidence. And, yes, the importance of knowing your genetic tendencies for certain diseases is a worthy draw as well. "Knowledge is power," as the saying goes. I could gain power over my foe. I had many check marks on the correct side of an imaginary chart I created. Let's just settle this and move on.

What if, on the other hand, I discovered the opposite? Still, isn't knowledge power in this case? A friend of mine tried to coerce me to test. "Wouldn't it be fun to investigate all the new family members you might find? Think of how much you love big family gatherings. You might have a newly discovered sister living in your same city. You could meet for coffee and get to know each other."

The thought of gaining new connections tempted me a little, but the reverse—the thought of losing the current connections deterred me to a greater degree. I may gain a new half-sister, but my very *whole sister* would also decrease to a half. If I had a different father, it would mean that I had no full siblings anywhere in the world. My cousins would decrease even more, for no bloodline would exist between us.

And my favorite aunt would have no genetic link to me whatsoever.

How would I tell my family? How could I break this news to my niece and nephew that their beloved grandpa was not my biological father after all and, therefore, the blood relation between us is diluted. All the talk of how we can see my nephew's face in all of my dad's childhood pictures. Still true, but how that connects the two of us in a profound way would disintegrate like the fade-out feature on live film. And what about friends? All of my Italian friends who bond with me over shared heritage? What about many of my colleagues who come to me for culinary advice? It's silly, but this potential embarrassment heated up inside. I desperately wanted my sister to stay my full sister. That snake coiled in the pit of my belly like it owns the place raised its head at these thoughts and questioned, "Do you really want to wake me now?"

On a whim, in a moment of abandon, I spit in the vial I had finally purchased a month before. Just sealed it up and threw the package in the mailbox. Commands came out of nowhere. Get it over with. Learn the truth. Imagine the relief. Let's conquer this fear.

I know the reason for my fear of a specific ride popular at old carnivals. One called the Rotor. I mean I vividly remember the particular incident that birthed this fear. Way back when I was about nine years old, kids frequented street fairs that came around to a school or church parking lot once a year or so. While waiting in line with a view of the ride, I watched the youngsters ahead already enjoying their turn. Standing against the wall as the Rotor began to twirl, the kids would stick to the wall by centrifugal force. And the floor would then drop, suspending all above nothing below, spinning round and round.

On this occasion, I watched in horror as one girl did not stick. She shrieked as she slowly slid down the wall while the floor dropped. The problem—the floor eventually comes back up. As it rose, it was crumpling her into awkward contortions. I did not understand the physics at this point and imagined that she was going to be sliced or crushed in some way as the floor seemed to have a mind of its own trying to return to position. And the ride keeper did not notice the difference between her scream and all the other screams of merriment, so he never stopped the ride. The girl kept screaming, and I exited the line. I never once rode the Rotor in all my following years of attending fairs. It became a real beast in my mind.

I guess I have to admit—a few fears *have* chased me through life, hiding behind corners and pouncing out at weakened times. A recurring nightmare has made it so that I cannot stand the sheets or blankets to touch my neck. The lightest material resting above my shoulders feels weighted and heavy enough to choke me. I picture trying to unravel a scarf tied too tightly around me and finding it knotted. Stifling. The more I try to untie, the tighter the knot.

A panic attack can put you into this type of frenzy.

20

Searching for my Name

And that's how I felt reading the map of my ancestry. Eastern Europe, Poland, Germanic Europe, Sweden, France, Denmark. Sweat beaded as I confirmed that no part of that beautiful boot was highlighted in the least.

Let me, I thought, investigate these family trees that subscribing members publish on the site and look for some recognizable surnames. You can digitally private message DNA matches on the ancestry site as well. So I sent out a few feelers:

"Hey, I notice we are related. Where are you from?" Or, "Do you know of any Giuseppes in your family tree?" Honest questions poured out, hoping the results were somehow inaccurate. "I always thought I was Italian, but I do not see any Italian matches. Am I missing something?" All who answered led me down proverbial rabbit holes. I grasped at minutely shaded regions, like maybe the area at the very tip of Italy, like Slovenia or on the other side where France touches the top near Switzerland? Maybe my dad was not as Italian as he thought. How accurate are these shadings anyway? Could there be a mistake? I never did find any long-lost Italians buried under the other European matches. I never found one person who knew any Giuseppe relatives.

At some point, the memory of my sister mentioning the fact that my mom's lover had many children burst forth from the back of my mind and marched straight to the front, giving fuel to my search. I plowed forward and messaged a "close relation" on the list because I saw a Polish last name in her lineage. She had not yet added all of her siblings' names to her family tree, but in our correspondence, I learned that she had seven brothers and sisters, and her father was from the same general area of Detroit as my family. The engine that seemed present in my belly was running non-stop, letting out exhaust in the form of nausea or heartburn quite often in the days that followed. I also matched with this person's first cousin on the DNA site, and I knew well all cousins of my mom and dad, so this new cousin could only be from a newly discovered biological father. The more I searched, the more I panicked. A familiar sense of dread rose as the room began to spin. I could feel the floor giving out below me, and I was not sticking securely to the wall as designed.

The reason I spit in the vial in the first place was to put that beastly suspicion to rest and confirm the truth that I had been telling myself for years now—that my mom was sure that my dad was my bloodline, and I had simply let this fear take over and grow too large.

The close relative, aka half-sister, with whom I was in frequent correspondence now, had no idea how we came to be related so directly but enjoyed chatting about possible relatives who could be the common thread. She was either in denial, like I had been, or truly did not process fully how it could be possible that the percentage of our shared DNA was so high. We were not *distant* relatives. By now, I knew it had to be her father who linked us but could not bring myself to come out and tell her, demolishing all of her illusions about her father. How would she handle that explosion of news this late in life? She did not choose or expect to face this reality;

she had tested only to find her lineage for fun. Now she not only has a half sibling to contend with but a revelation about her father she may wish to keep locked away. She soon arranged for an in-person meeting to share some pictures of what she assumed were distant relatives of mine, and I was all about seeing some faces and finding a tangible connection.

Would I feel something immediately? Would my spirit just know when I saw this woman, like stories I had heard about long-lost, genetic relations? Would finding this connection alleviate the pain of cutting off the flow of blood and, therefore, blocking so many of the links in my world prior to this point?

Part III

You who felt yourself so different from

Everyone but me

Remain the same

Hearts return from whence they came

21

Our Father

Sitting in the Panera across from Maria, I study my new-found sister's eyes. She's quite a bit older than I am. I cannot see any resemblance here. I feel no connection. She talks of her mother for a bit, and my mind wanders. Why would I want to hear about her *mother*? The table shakes from my unintentional, constant bouncing leg. My stomach does jumping jacks, and I may have to run to the restroom. She brings up some uncle that she lost track of over the years, as if he might be our link in the broken chain she can't quite figure out that makes us so closely related. But what she does not know is that my sister remembered my mom's lover's first name, and it is indeed Maria's father.

The photos of her father show him at various ages through the years before his death long before this meeting. I try to hide the slight shaking of my hands as I slowly shuffle through them, hoping sweat and oil will not smudge them. I look at this man's eyes. The smile on his face. Where the smile lines appear. The shape of his mouth. As I quietly stare at these pictures of this man named Jan, avoiding direct eye-contact with Maria, understanding begins to dawn on her face. She looks right into me . . .with a kind grin emerging.

"Unless," she begins. "You are my *sister*," she finally says, a beam shining from her eyes. I nod my head in tentative confirmation, happy that she got there on her own and I did not have to tear the blinders off her eyes myself.

"I always suspected my dad was having an affair. I can't say I'm surprised by this news," she says, with her smile remaining. This news does not deliver a sucker punch from which she has to recover the way I have to.

How? I wonder. How did my mom find time with this man without her family knowing either? How did no one suspect that her surprise baby came from this man? Or if they did suspect, how was everyone so adept at the keeping of that secret, as if they were trained in covert operations? If my dad knew, how could he have so fully accepted another man's child as his own? His reputation was not one as some altruistic man of sacrifice. That would be difficult for any man.

And while my mom was admitting her truth to me all those years ago, why lie at that point about her "hundred percent" conviction that Jan was not my biological father? And why all the references to my Italian blood? Was that my mom trying to convince herself? Do I believe that my sister does not know to this day? Is this why my brother never seemed to like me growing up? Is it possible that he suspected I was not fully theirs?

All of these questions swirled within my head like the whirlpools we used to make in our small, above-ground swimming pool by running hard around the edges in one direction and watching the middle tunnel form, sucking all the dirt to that center. All of the dirty questions from the last twenty years were being pulled from the edges as well and collected right there in the middle of everything. I am under water for part of this conversation. I hear her through saturated ear canals. She is somewhat joyful.

120

"Oh I can't wait to show you more of our pictures. You look like *our father*."

Our father? He's not my father, but I am not fit to appear rude or unkind.

"Your grandfather is a famous artist, you know? We own some of his renowned photography from the late 1800s."

Photography? That can't be a gene passed down, can it, but I am something like a photographer myself, and my daughter really is one. People have always said we had an eye for the craft. My daughter makes a living in the profession. Crazy, but the Ancestry website *does* offer a section with some "personality traits" that are likely to be present in an individual based on her DNA. Mine goes into such detail as to tell me I probably enjoy dance and art. Interesting, my daughter's biological great grandfather has art on display in some old Detroit buildings, among other places. A tiny seed of curiosity buds from deep within.

"I would like to see some of this art," I say.

I do not fully understand why I say this, but it seems a previously unknown grandfather, especially from a distance, is easier to examine than a whole different father, as if the new one would somehow cancel out my real one.

She proceeds, "Our father was loved by everybody. The life of the party. So talented in many different areas. A real personality. I miss him so much. He lived well into his 80s, ya know? Loved his Polish sweets, though. Pastries every day."

"I'm sure he would have met you at some point in your life. He could never have let a child of his go unnoticed. Do you think you may have met him as a child?" she prods.

No memory appears. I can't splice anything together about meeting another man as a child. I do not know why I want to know, but I want to know what he did for a living. Did he laugh a lot? Did he love nature? My fascination with genetics bubbling just a little. Apparently, he was quite intelligent. Successful at many things, and an engineer by vocation. Great at math. That tickles me; I am not a fan of math. English and language arts for me all the way. I collect all of these facts about him and stick them in my purse for safe keeping. And that's what they are—just facts. Not connections. Not little genes dotting the twists of my DNA. I am interested in seeing the pictures but feel no kinship. I do not look into his eyes and see myself at all. This reaction does not seem in accordance with stories I have heard about adopted children meeting their biological parents later in life and immediately closing some long-untied gap. Some have always felt out of place, and when faced with genetic relatives, describe some magnetic pull. This experience just feels like a story of another family's life. Something you might see in a Lifetime movie. But I *am* curious about these siblings.

A half-brother is out there somewhere, and I was never that close to *my* real brother. I remember him shooing me away whenever I tried army-crawling into the campout tents he often made by throwing an expansive tarp over a clothesline in our backyard on humid summer nights. Sleeping bags layered atop the grass and an extension cord trailing to the garage outlet allowing for his little box television set made for a comfortable escape from our stuffy house that lacked air conditioning. The peaceful glow out there lured me, but I was never invited to stay. He might toss out to me what looked like a miniature tissue box with tiny, light pink papers to play with. I could pull a sheet out and let the paper dissolve on my tongue for the hint of cherry flavoring. I had no idea what these rolling papers were then, but I now suspect that this could have been his reason for barring me from the tent. Perhaps this new brother was different. Maybe he's more welcoming and talkative. For a while, every time I walked the aisle of the grocery store or sat in a crowded restaurant, I looked more deeply into the faces of the patrons than I ever did before. I kept thinking, that man could be my brother, or that woman could be my sister.

But for some reason, as happy as Maria is about her new-found sister, she does not want to share me with the rest of the seven siblings. She does not want them to know. Apparently, this knowledge that their beloved father had an affair would crush them, though it does not crush, or even surprise, her. I guess I wonder about the right to my secret; is it only mine? Can I unravel someone else's secret without their permission? I am afraid to push it with Maria. Like I would betray her trust if I went searching out these other relatives on my own. And my searching somehow feels like a betrayal to my original siblings too. It feels like it diminishes our relationship despite the hasty reassurance thrown out from a couple of friends:

"Your sister is still your sister no matter what. You grew up together. You have the same mom. Who cares who the DNA came from. You're still you."

But in some ways, I am not me. I am not the youngest daughter in an Italian family. I did not inherit my skin tone from my father or those traits that made me a great cook. I

123

do not walk like Norm with my feet turned out to the side, or display the calm wit passed down from his side of the family. The many times I have gazed at my children's faces and seen traces of my father's face are now counterfeit. All of my cousins seemed to have vanished. Even my last name is somewhat of a lie. Though legal, it does not reflect my heritage.

I cannot seem to grab hold of a new ethnicity when I never held it growing up. I *want* to tell my friend, Mary Jane, that I am now Polish, or I guess I always was, but I cannot seem to open that box. I keep it sealed with my secret folded safely inside.

In some strange reasoning, I feel as if my sister and I stay full sisters as long as she never looks inside that box. Our conversations of paternity or of my mom's past abruptly came to an end with my sister assuming I would never investigate further than asking her those few questions that one time. It is not a topic she cares about and so she figures I don't care either. She could never fathom the gut punch I endured in my little research endeavor.

22

Family Tree

I think back to elementary school—somewhere around the fifth grade. The teacher assigned a pretty extensive family tree project. This would require some detailed research. It was long before my cousins compiled that handy booklet for the Giuseppe family reunions. I would not be able to pull out that list to help fill in the template for this project. My mom's mother, named Maletta and called Gramma Mal for short, had always enjoyed watching me thoughtfully go through her box of old photos every time we visited her down in Florida where she and my grandpa retired.

The sepia color and thick photo paper felt less delicate than photos today. More permanent, especially considering how few are printed these days. And compared to our storage of them on our phones or in *Facebook* folders. Now after viewing photos once or twice, we can lose track of them, so many thousands of snapshots.

These pictures stacked in one cardboard box, however, dated back to the late 1800s. I had these faces memorized by my careful cataloging of the photos each year of my childhood, and the tactile memory of this activity remains today. Knowing how much I loved these photographs, Gramma Mal willed that box to me to cherish long after her death. In preparation, long before her time to go, she carefully labeled the portraits in my presence and with my mom's help. In blue ballpoint pen, these names are still visible, and I am assured of the direct connections written on the back of each relative's face. I can see clearly on just which sturdy branch each one perches. The shape of my smile matches exactly that of my great-great grandmother's. And still, each day, I pass by her framed portrait on my antique sofa table in my home. Going through the exercise of labeling and studying these family members over and over helped me tell a story and display one side of a beautiful branching tree for my elementary school project.

The other side of the tree would take more investigative effort, though, since Grandma Giuseppe had never let me file through her many photos during my childhood. Mom and dad took me for a special visit to Grandpa and Grandma Giuseppe's house with my notebook in hand for this research in fifth grade. I would have to do my own writing of the names of relatives and determine where they sat in our tree. Grandma did have a plethora of photos pasted to the knotty-pine paneled wall in the basement in somewhat of a montage; no order of descendants neatly diagrammed there, but it was interesting to peruse the copious pictures. Photos of children laughing or couples marrying and feeding each other cake. Babies in frilly christening dresses held over the baptismal font. Old blurry faces you would have to strain your eyes to identify. We spent some time looking at that wall and figuring out who was who and where I fit. Sliding off the crinkly, shiny, kelly-green faux-leather seat in the basement, I set my notebook and pencil down right on the matching green and white speckled vinyl floor, not worrying much about its preservation at the moment. After a little work for this school project, Grandma set me up at the kitchen table with a bowl of fresh raspberries from her bush along the fence and thick cream poured over top. Afterward, I could join the adults outside and run around the yard with the rich flavors still lingering around my tastebuds, and that was more fun than writing names in my notebook.

Detroit plots were typically a 40 X 100-foot piece of land, if that much, and sodded green with perhaps a border of flowers and shrubs marking the perimeter. My grandparents got lucky, and a whole street around their block was never developed, so they had a long, narrow yard the length of the missing houses that should have been behind them. My grandfather planted rows and rows of vegetables bricked in with precise garden sections on each side of a long, grassy path down the middle. In the summer, we could pick beans and cucumbers from the wooden lattices Grandpa posted for their need to climb. Hiding in the tall corn stalks was a favorite pastime, for "knee-high by the fourth of July" meant a tall man's knee, not a little girl's height. Running past his workshop in the garage, leaving the scent of sawdust and cedar behind, you would find yourself at the end of that path under a trellis of grapevines. Shiny green grapes. Now and then, mom would pluck one from up high and sneak it to me before anyone noticed. Sour were these stolen gems, sometimes making our eyes water. The white wood-slatted fence in the back, separating Grandpa's yard from the neighbor's, enclosed a white billy goat, sporting the predictable spikey, tufted goatee, just like the Gruff's illustrations in the Norwegian folktale. We liked to feed him a handful of clover or grass and some little pieces of carrots from the garden that was still producing through September. Mom always called our stocky goat friend, Little Willy.

I left my grandparents' house with a list of relatives in descending order to pencil onto my poster-board-sized family tree at home. Careful with the spelling of some of these long surnames with many consonants, I proudly filled in my background. My lineage. Quickly pasting down photographs before a soft breeze coming through the window might blow them all out of place. My budding interest in history emerging as I learned where I came from. How my family emigrated from Introdacqua, Italy, north of Rome, across the ocean to West Virginia in the late 1800s. How my dad grew up in the woods and the mountains playing barefoot outside all the day long as a child. Hunting pheasant or rabbits for his mother's stew. And how some members of my family remained in West Virginia while a few others moved to Detroit for work, my grandparents, for example. I heard the story of my dad dating my mom's older sister as teenagers, and then after spending a couple of years away for work, coming back to visit and finding my mom all grown up and more than eager for a courtship. Luckily, her sister had moved on and was about to marry her beau, so giving up Norm for Doris' sake posed no ill feelings. Doris and Norm married in 1950, just a year later. This was my story. I presented it with pride to my fifth-grade class, pronouncing the names articulately and memorizing them for all time.

Years later, when I perused the booklet at the Giuseppe family reunion before I was sure of my lineage, the information seemed to close some gaps and make room for branching shoots growing farther from the trunk and spraying out, displaying more relatives than I knew, wondering what similarities might be among us from DNA that, like magnetic strips, drew us together, linking even future generations. My cousin Donna had asked if I'd like to join her on a trip to our ancestors' home in Italy and walk the villages to feel the kinship of the place. She had gone once and simply knocked on doors of neighbors whose families had stayed in this village for generations. Imagine her delight at meeting a distant relative in this manner.

She still brings it up every so often: "Let's go and do this again," she implores. "You need to feel this. You need to look into the eyes of kin and touch the hand of a person who sat in your tree all this time and is ready to leave only her name behind for descendants to remember as she leaves this earth. For now, she is real. Not just a name on paper. She would like a glimpse of the ones who come after her. Like you and me. Please come with me, Cuz."

Donna never saw what a fierce storm had rolled in, striking my tree's limbs. She had no way of knowing that the fallen branches lay haphazardly all over my yard by now.

23

An Imposter

I now choke on the response to the question too often posed of background: "What ethnicity are you, Michelle?" Or again, the assumption, "You're Italian, right? How do you make that pasta sauce everyone calls 'Liquid Gold'?" Just today, at my exercise class, a woman, in a thick European accent, blurted out the question: "Are you Italian? The country I come from borders Italy, and you look just like all the Italians over there." What? Why would someone think this looking at me? All my life I breezed past these statements and never thought twice about my answers. Now, I stutter and feel deceptive when I come up with a way to change the subject or get around the lie.

"Yes, my dad was Italian." I might say, "He taught me to cook" if the question relates to food.

"I was raised in an Italian home." That does it for a time. What ethnicity am I? "Oh I guess I am like my mom always described herself—a Heinz 57. A bit of this and that." I am afraid my face will expose the truth as if I am guilty. An imposter. I resist eye contact, so a trained professional would pick out the tell in my body language in an instant. But these questions do not come from trained professionals, and I brush past the topics without anyone catching me raking dirt with a branch behind me to cover my tracks.

I have wished from the moment I received the results that I could have a re-do. I try to turn around and go the opposite way, but the whirlpool's current I have created is too strong, and pushing in the opposite direction is just impossible in my weakness. Why did I listen to friends who told me to go ahead and test? They thought it would be satisfying to know the truth, but I most emphatically believe I would be better off not knowing. I could have lived the rest of my life with a bit of suspicion on one side of the chart but many more checks on the right side of my tally that confirmed I was indeed biologically connected to my dad as much as spiritually. I felt Italian, and, therefore, I was. Before DNA tests became popular, my dad was just my dad. Knowledge is *not* power for me; it is simply a burden to carry, and so far, I am as adept at keeping this secret as my mom was of hers for so many years.

About the time my eldest daughter was three or four years old, a story hit the airways. An adoptive family had a little girl the same age as my Kate. The girl's birth mother wanted to reverse her decision and take her daughter back. My friends and I listened to the adoptive mother's interview, sorrow emanating from her face as she described the real possibility of this adoption being overturned. A horrifying thought. Could the courts really decide in favor of the biological mother despite the permanent attachment that had already exchanged between this little girl and her parents. Imagine all the sleepless nights rocking this baby and caring for her when she was sick or hungry. The essential bonding. All the joy at the little milestones as she grew into a toddler and spoke her first words, "Mama" and "Dada." How confusing for this girl to start over. The woman pleaded her case: the adoption was legal, and the child was thriving. She was cemented in as part of this family. Video footage played across the screen of the child squealing and laughing as her daddy pushed her on the swing set and chased her around the yard. Appeals to the judge came from others following the case as well. Biology is not the *only* aspect of parenthood. This is not such a simple verdict as to whom this child belonged.

At this time, I had no seeds of suspicion growing in me about my own father. My mother had not yet disclosed her secret, nor had she ever hinted that I was not fully a Giuseppe by birth. I had no experience with adoption either, or the bonding process that must occur between adoptive parents and children. I just knew the cord that bound my child and me had grown so strong in her first few years of life, and even desperate, that my empathy lay with the adoptive mother who had nurtured this girl since birth. The attachment to my daughter was not simply because she came from my own body; I just knew that I had held her since day one, and I was sure I would feel this same connection to her whether or not she came from me. Even if I found that she was not my biological child by some mistake, I would never want to give her up. I identified with this adoptive mother's plight so deeply that I bordered on an obsessive preoccupation with the story on the news. I held my daughter's hand more tightly as I watched this mother on television have her baby ripped from her embrace and taken to a new home with a new family, for the judge, indeed, did side with the biological mother and nullified this adoption. How would this little girl adjust to her new family members, even if they were biological, for she only knew these other parents as her own?

I found myself weeping over the case, though it had nothing to do with me. The brokenness the adoptive parents and the little girl felt was too much. I still think of the situation today. How a person must feel when the ground beneath her quakes and she finds herself separated from those she loves, those who started her on her path. Does she search for them forever? I presume we all adjust to these cataclysmic events, but they shape us still. And we certainly understand the repercussions of such an earthquake's damage when we see it at age fifty rather than during early childhood when we only have a vague sense of where all the debris landed in the storm.

Many times, in my childhood when I just wanted to get away from metaphorically strengthening winds blowing by, I would find myself sitting on a fallen log settled across the swamp in our woods thinking. Taking deep breaths and listening to the sounds in the trees. Birds flitting about. Trickling water. Bugs. I did not know about meditative breathing creating the desired effect of slowing down that flight-or-fight response at the time, but it sure happened to me even without the scientific knowledge. If some sort of storm in life threatened me, I would just rest here and lean down close to the water, hovering, and watch the world of the polliwogs. Collecting those little overexcited swimmers in a jar and knowing that they would transform into toads, for I had watched that first-hand display of science many times, somehow grounded me in a reality that things would always change and get better. I could weather a storm or two, looking forward to the sunshine that would eventually break through and encourage growth and transformation. I was now in another storm as an adult, frantically looking for my dad's blue sedan in the rain, for him to give me some assurance that I would make it out, but he was gone.

At fifteen years old, I took my drivers' training course, perhaps, a little more seriously than most of my peers. The instructor showed a movie of a young-man-turned-paraplegic after crashing into a tree without wearing a seatbelt and, therefore, catapulting through the windshield. And that film secured a lasting impression and accomplished its purpose for this new driver. Images flashed across the screen of the seat where the boy would have been left had he been fastened in place. It was completely intact. He would have been fine had he not hit the glass.

I always wore my safety belt after that even though it was sort of a new idea for the rest of my family. I don't think it was a law in the 1970s. I remember having to search and yank out the belts that had been shoved into the creases of the seats. During my permit driving practice with my dad coaching me, I listened to his calm instructions. "Ease over to the next lane while keeping your foot on the gas. None of this sudden switching from one lane to another," he said with abrupt hand gestures imitating the car weaving unsteadily. It's funny how I can still hear his voice all these years later when I drive along the highway.

One recording often on repeat in my mind comes from my overly cautious stopping at a red light that was almost a run right through because I was nervous about the driver behind me. He didn't look like he was slowing down enough and might bump into me if I stopped suddenly at the light. As my eyes went back and forth from what was in front of me to the rearview mirror, my dad emphatically urged me to stop. "Don't worry about what's behind you. That guy will take care of himself. Your job is to keep your eyes ahead of you. That's more important. You have a little more control over that. You can see what's coming and avoid hitting people." I still wanted to pump my brakes, signaling for that tailgater to slow down.

"But what if he does hit me? He looks like he's going to. Then what?"

"And then what is right. You can't control him. You can only control yourself. Chances are he won't hit you, but if he does, it will likely be just a little tap. It'll wake him up. But the consequences are much higher if you run through a light ahead of yourself. That would be a lot worse for you. The drivers behind you are like the past. They are not your responsibility. You can't influence them—you can't change what they do."

Every time I come to a red light and find myself tempted to check my rearview mirror, I hear my dad telling me not to worry about what's behind me. The past will take care of itself.

Who knew my driver's training would be a metaphor for my life. I still worry about the past and want to slow it all down, pump the breaks and warn everyone to stop. I want to go back and tell people not to push me into DNA testing.

136

Stop letting the past barrel right into me. Keep it back there in its place.

My dad had banked on the chances being low that a tap from behind would be anything other than a fender bender. But that feared bump from the guy behind me manifested as a true collision that left me unable to drive forward. Somehow the damage to the back made it difficult to steer, knocking me off my path. It broke my confidence. It changed me.

The young driver whose life altered drastically when he crashed through his windshield remembers that moment— that decision not to wear a safety belt. He forever separates his life into two hemispheres: before the accident and after. He had to learn a new way of life. Life from a wheelchair. What would he do with it? He would advise people that you can't change the past. You must move forward even if in a new reality.

24

Standing in Front of a Mirror

There comes a point in everyone's life, perhaps, where we wonder who we really are at the core. How did we become this person? Do we inherit important traits from our parents at birth no matter who raises us? I remember hearing a story long ago, perhaps on a talk show, about two twin boys separated at birth and adopted by different families across the country from each other. When the families got in touch about eight years later, they shared stories of raising these two boys. One mom expressed frustration over the fact that her son would only eat oatmeal if she sprinkled cinnamon all over it. The other mom laughed. She had always thought it endearing that her little boy loved cinnamon so much that she joyfully sprinkled it on his morning cereal to satisfy his craving. Were these boys born with a love of the spice? Is our personality, our likes and dislikes, or our desires destined? Written into our genes from the start? Or does the sum of our life's experiences create our being?

I do not know why it matters exactly where my genetics originated. But it does. The idea that I was designed by the Creator of the universe found its way into my spirit long ago and glided around the confines of my brain since I was very young, and that's quite unexplainable since faith was never fostered by my parents. This belief has never been extinguished, even by years of science classes or the modern philosophies I sat under at universities. Later, I learned the beautiful name *Elohim* and all of the power packed in that title for God. Yahweh—just breath with added vowels for some type of human understanding. The fact that I wrestle so often with this little demon of knowledge about my origin now, therefore, baffles me. In the few years that I have known the truth, I have constantly felt an unraveling—like I am dropping important parts of myself along a path. Realizing the loss now and then, I stop, turn, and try to pick up a piece to reattach; however, the limb or appendage will not fit just right and allow the proper blood flow to be workable anymore. These pieces are all just precariously hanging there, barely holding on—maybe not visible to just any passer-by but quite obvious to me when I stand in front of a mirror.

My mom used to describe the shock she felt when she would catch a glimpse of herself in a store window at times later in life. She walked around believing she was who she was in her head, but when she saw this aged person reflected, she stopped, startled. "Is that what I really look like? Is that who I have become? I kept picturing myself the way I looked when I was 35. But *this* person is old."

Old, yes, but mom could eventually come around and say, "Look, *she* is still there if I search deep into her eyes. I see her mother. I see her father, yes. There she is."

That startle is happening to me two-fold these days. For my whole life, I thought I was someone specific. Michelle. Italian. Daughter of Norm and Doris. Hints of my aunt in me. Qualities of my grandmother passed down to my first-born daughter. The look of my cousins in my next daughter. The flash of my dad's expressions in my newborn grandbaby's smile. But then I stop short in front of a store window and notice that all of that has disappeared. Reality has bullied my imagination into submission.

Sometimes I pull out my parents' old photo albums I have stowed away in plastic bins. And I mull over them, turning those aged black pages, hardly still bound by loose threads, to relive some of the old family memories. Smeared, golden glue trails that have lost their stickiness and old maroon corner tabs that have slid to the creases of the book remind me that these pictures are all out of place now. Black and white photographs of the three of us little newborn children can only be placed back in the correct order if you have memorized the babies in the photos, like I have. Those who will inherit these books after me will never know which baby goes where in the family album. And I don't know that anyone will take the time to dig out these tabs and reattach them anyway. Are grandchildren and great-grandchildren these days all that curious as to where they came from?

The Creator has allowed us to understand the biology of human life. We even have microscopic cameras that have enabled us to animate the whole process and development of a fetus in-utero. We can study heredity—the probability of inheriting a certain eye color or facial structure. These topics have always fascinated me. Like how two blue-eyed people could not possibly have a brown-eyed child. I wonder how many times that scientific fact caused questions to arise between a husband and a wife. I examined these subjects way back in my high school Anatomy & Physiology class, never dreaming for a moment that it related to my family at all, for I had greenish eyes just like my father. And I thought that it was my dad who may have had another child out there somewhere, not my mom who held such a secret so expertly bound down in the deepest dungeon that none of us heard the truth whispering its existence, coming up through the floor vents.

I am created, yes, but all the science the Creator set in motion for the miraculous process was done in secret, shrouded in deception. Sure, it all happened in the traditional way of biology, but it did not occur in the backseat of our Buick or on the family vacation in Canada with husband and wife, mom and dad. And I do not get the satisfaction of knowing anything about this interloper and if he loved my mother, or if he even knew of my creation at all. I don't even know if my mother knew. Was she lying to me when she told me she was a hundred percent certain that my dad was indeed my father? Was she lying every time she told her story of my conception with her little chuckle following? Perhaps the story was all for my dad's benefit. Maybe she found herself pregnant, and she swiftly seduced my dad so she could tell that salacious rendition of how she ended up with child just after my dad thought it almost impossible but took the chance anyway. I would like to give my mom the benefit of the doubt and land on the idea that she really did not know, but a recent memory has just recently bubbled up, and it gives me pause.

Young enough for my mom to still carry me on her hip, I see myself in her arms with the view of the bowling alley around me. She tried several times to pass me off to a strange man to hold me for a minute, encouraging me to happily sit in this man's arms. I, of course, did not want to and protested with the strong will I still possess. With an adult analysis, I think, *why would a young child want any man she didn't know to hold her at all?* I hear my mom's voice saying, "Nope. She doesn't want to," as she pulled me back from his arms.

A tea-colored, female cardinal landed on the post of my deck as I was relaxing in the sun, paying me a rare, personal visit. She sat preening for a minute. Tilted her head and looked right at me as she let out a sweet musical phrase. I felt a flip in my belly and shivered despite the heat, as if my mom was trying to tell me something. But I am not adept at decoding melodies. And the visit was short-lived.

.

25

Tiny Seeds Planted

In my early teenage years before a love for literature began shooting up sturdy, green tendrils in me, I had a hard time coming in from the woods to enjoy reading for long periods of time. One year, my English teacher assigned a whole not-so-short novel to read over spring break, and my mom and I had spent that time on Clearwater Beach in Florida. I made several attempts to log hours in this book, but suntan oil, saltwater, and gritty sand all over my hands do not make for a comfortable read. Besides, I could not see the pages very well through my dark sunglasses needed to cut the glare from a robust Florida sun. I had never been one to read on the beach, and I never saw that activity modeled either.

My mom was not an avid reader; although, I do appreciate the fond memory of her reading to me from a collection of traditional fairy tales in a hard cover book kept on a shelf in the hall linen closet, right on top of hastily folded sheets, next to one other pink canvas-covered medical book I enjoyed reading as well. I still display the Fairy Tale book in my home, so happy I held onto it after my parents passed. I noticed this vintage collector's item is about ninety-five dollars to buy it used today. My old copy is tattered and falling apart, and I rarely let anyone touch it as it sits behind glass, the cover exhibiting the perfect rendition of my childhood—a fairy and a sprite sitting atop a fatty toadstool telling stories to three eager-eyed children, little elves peeking around the smaller mushrooms in the wood. Rumpelstiltskin's conniving ways captured my attention much more than this novel due for sophomore English class.

By the time we were on our way home from Florida, the panic began percolating. I would not be able to read this novel before returning to class on Monday. I harbored anger toward my otherwise favorite teacher for assigning a book I did not think I liked anyway. Mom encouraged me to practice driving on I-75 since I would be turning sixteen soon and getting my full driver's license. She planned to rest in the backseat as I covered some of the 1200 miles going north. With her flaking lipstick covering only the outline of her lips and her over-permed hair clumping up to reveal patches of her scalp, mom sat up, disheveled, and saw my book sliding around the back window ledge. She rubbed her sleepy eyes and realized that I had not read any on our trip, so she picked it up and offered to read aloud as I drove.

This worked wonders. Mom changed her voice for each character and read with such expression that we began to notice the wit and intelligence in this writing. Some characters remained dull and unlikable, while others spoke with quirky southern accents. Oops. Neither mom nor I realized at the time that *Emma*, by Jane Austen, was British literature, so no characters would have sounded like they were from Alabama in reality, but this whimsey kept me focused nonetheless. Who would have predicted my love for Austen later in life when I taught Brit Lit to high schoolers, performing various character voices, not southern ones mind you, reading aloud, hoping to draw in my students to the story. I would like to use the familiar head palm emoji here, and I cannot help but chuckle with complete tenderness as I recall my mom doing this for me. Just as she also used to type my school essays back when we all hand wrote first and then had to peck out the sentences on the old clunky machines. Her secretarial work trained her to type like a mad woman. We expected steam to rise from the keys. It was not until well into college that I worked in the writing center and learned to type as I thought on the boxy tabletop computer using a word processor called *Galahad*. The memories of mom helping me in these ways are ones I keep on record and, often, draw the needle back, setting it gently down again and again to listen to her voice whenever I need to. Tiny seeds planted for who I would become.

26

Who Can Calm the Storm

Why does this newly-born, so-called identity crisis tease my mind, taunting me like a bully on the school bus back in Detroit? I would like to rest and stay grounded in the truth that I am who I always was. But I am not, in a way. I have had to sever certain ties, and that leaves me drifting. Sometimes the waves are higher than other times. Carrying the secret. Holding it tight to my chest like it's some delicate artifact seems to make the waves more noticeable, just like you hit every pothole in a car when you are trying not to spill your hot coffee. If I get distracted for an instant, I am afraid I'll drop it. And once it breaks, there will be no putting it back together.

Who am I really? And what made me who I am? And how can I keep it all hidden? Must I continuously shovel sand on top of a sink hole or bail out water that keeps filling up? I am not strong enough to do that forever. At a recent stay in a hotel, the artwork at eye level was the inside view of the bow of a boat pointing toward the shore. Once you lose yourself in the eye-line, you feel movement as if you are swaying atop the water. I suppose the artist meant for a sense of hope and beauty, not the never-ending feeling of rocking and drifting, unable to reach that dry land. But I am learning that I might be able to call on that One who commands the storms, just as he did in a famous gospel story. I want to call out and ask him to do it again, for me.

We all play out that Bible story in many scenarios, don't we? I picture myself in a boat with friends during a ferocious storm, yelling at everyone to get their life jackets on and directing them where to sit while Jesus lays back, peacefully sleeping. Clouds and winds ramping up to engulf us in one of those dark furies. And we have the man on board who commands the very weather. Emmanuel. God with us. Would I forget to ask him for help, thinking I could navigate the boat on my own? I might tell everyone on board where to sit for the most effective weight balance and express disappointment when they do not seem to know the best way to help. Like,

"Hey, scoop up some of this water and dump it off the sides perhaps." I might not want to bother Jesus with the task of dominating this storm, even though he *is* sitting right there with us. I forget in the turmoil that he can walk above the waves. Even better, he called one of his disciples to walk on water too. What takes over in my mind, instead, is that Peter sunk right away, so I am afraid to try to jump out of this boat onto "solid ground." What if I sink too? I already feel like I *am* sinking and flailing my arms about in this same story. I know he *can* pull me out, but will he choose to? What if I drown down here?

If I could just get a look at His countenance, I would gain some confidence. I would slosh over the boat's watery bottom, pellets of rain hitting me in the face, and just grab onto Him. He is the only one who can demand the ominous storm clouds to stand down. I might see bits of light as the sun peeks from behind a heavy barrier, asserting its warm dominance over the darkness. That same sun reflected in his eyes.

I hear a gentle voice, as if whispered on a breeze, "Michelle, Peter only sank when he took his eyes off the incarnate Lord, El Elyon, God Most High. Omnipotent."

27

Out of Miry Clay

Birds evoke symbolic meaning to people, especially in times of stress or grief. The lore surrounding cardinals, for instance, is ancient, possibly passed down from the Native Americans. A common belief is that if the bird visits you, it is carrying the spirit of a departed loved one. Doves symbolize peace or maybe, more specifically, hard times coming to a resolution. Perhaps these beliefs are better described as feelings. Feelings that spring up from our core when we are missing a person, and right at the deepest moment of sadness, a bird lands in front of you and cocks its head just so, like my pale cardinal.

I have always loved doves. I imagine the type depicted in Biblical art. A bird with smooth, white plumes and a sprig of an olive branch poking out the side of his beak. The ultimate sign of peace, showing Noah that it was safe to leave the ark after the long wait for the waters to recede, to move forward, to step onto solid ground. Begin your life again, start over, the bird intimated.

Years ago, when death was lurking awfully close to my mom, in a moment of weakness, I asked God for a sign. I usually avoid such bold requests—partly because I hold some memory from childhood that says we should not tempt God that way, as if He's a magician of sorts. But another part of me wonders if I avoid asking for signs because I doubt. . . and then what will I do with the silence I might encounter when God chooses not to provide me such a clear and perfect answer? It is easier to assign our own meaning to a bird visitation than it is to ask for one to occur and deal with disappointment if it doesn't.

But my mom was slipping away, and I kept ruminating over all my unanswered questions. We had never revisited the fifteen-year relationship she confessed to and when it began or when it ended. Or if my dad knew of this affair. Or if the man knew of my conception. Mom and I never had time for such discussion because her last years of life after my dad passed away were filled with hospital visits, home care, alternative trials for cirrhosis of the liver. Preparing for my mom's imminent death began the day after my dad's funeral. Her liver was so damaged that doctors told us it would never repair itself. She likely had a few months to live. My husband and I managed a little make-shift room off the back of our house that, thankfully, included a private bathroom. We brought my mom to our home to live out the rest of her days with us to prevent her dying alone in a nursing facility, but we had to accept the fact that my mom would indeed die in our home. And this would be no easy situation.

Each morning, as I descended the stairs to check on her, I mentally steeled myself to find her lying there emptied of her spirit, her life. Images of her dead body in my house always found their way into my mind in the early hours before dawn. I could only shoo them away by finding her awake, greeting me with that familiar voice, and laughter that remained even as she knew the state of her disease. Sometimes I sent my husband downstairs first to report back to me whether or not I could face the morning. Mom was a pleasant patient, and very grateful for our care, calling me Dr.

Michelle. But these months zapped my energy, and I was completely exhausted.

While my sister took some time caring for our mother, my husband and I drove down, once again, to Florida for a little respite. As husbands and wives often do, we found ourselves drifting into our own worlds. Craig was driving and I was watching the landscape whiz by like an arcade game with bright colors. The sun warmed my face through the windshield. I had no way of knowing how the suspicion of my ancestry would plague me later. At this point, I didn't even know to ask for help dealing with *that* trouble, but I just kept wondering how I was going to handle my mom's death so soon after my dad's. I already felt like an orphan since I had been catapulted into the role of nursemaid, more like the mother than the daughter. And I may have even been a little salty with God for placing me in this position, for I was the one in the family who struggled the most with my mom's alcoholism. I was the one forever trying to coerce her to stop drinking and go to Alcoholics Anonymous. And here I was— a primary caregiver and dealing with all the physical repercussions of the addiction. During those times in the past that I begged my parents to stop drinking for the sake of their health, both mom and dad would jokingly say, "Ya gotta die of something," as if this death would be like a heart attack that would one day take them out in a matter of minutes.

This death is no easy or quick course. The body bloats up, and an elderly woman can appear nine months pregnant. Several times, I sat with my mom in the hospital as they inserted a tube into her abdomen and let the other end hang like a garden hose, draining fluid into a bucket on the floor to give her some relief and help her breathe better for a short time. Until it filled up again. I would keep my eyes glued to a Home & Garden magazine during this process to try to appear unfazed, as if this were simply a routine procedure.

Mom also ended up having to take frequent insulin shots as the pancreas stubbornly shrugged its shoulders and gave up, defeated as well. Mom's skin tuned to decoupage, tearing at the slightest bump. I learned wound care too and could dress the weeping lacerations like it was my job. I guess it was my job. Her liver could not break down proteins anymore, so ammonia, a by-product left over, would travel up to her brain and float around, just as if she were drunk. As soon as her words began to slur and she forgot where she was, we would know the ammonia was too high, and she needed to flush her body of it quickly.

The treatment for this symptom is a nasty process that no one wants to live through. Force down this viscous liquid called Lactulose and stay close to the bathroom, as if you are prepping for a colonoscopy. Yes, she would be clear thinking again, but the quality of life was diminishing fast. Eventually my mom chose to stop taking the drug, knowing this would mean a sooner end, but she decided she would rather die than live in these conditions. No wonder I was tired—too tired to plan another funeral.

So in the car that day, on the way down to Florida, I asked God to give me some assurance that He would carry me through the death of my mother. Could I truly rest on this vacation and come home ready to deal with the reality of my plight. Maybe I could shore up some energy. Maybe God would provide peace. I saw a greyish brown dove fly over. . . or maybe it was a pigeon. That nudged my request:

God, could you show me a dove again on this trip to communicate that you are listening? And I don't care if it is a little tan one either. It doesn't have to be as elaborate as Noah's. If I see one fly by again, I'll take that as a sign.

Soon we stopped at a rest area and these thoughts left me for details of our trip. Checking into our hotel, finding restaurants, walking along the beach.

A few days in, we stopped at Silver Springs to watch some manatee and enjoy the famous glass-bottom boat ride. Tropical fish spiral underneath, modeling their colorful dress in a fashion show for patrons all day long. It is quite serene watching a heron fly over and land on the bank nearby.

Seeking some shade later in the day, we decided to sit under a pavilion for a predatory bird show. We were horrified as a falconer fed a hawk something that looked like a live mouse right before our eyes, parents quickly shielding children's faces. But seeing a bald eagle close enough to reach out and touch, leather tether straps swinging back and forth, is spectacular. Owls and Osprey are remarkable too, but I could do without the vultures. Not such a peaceful show, but definitely interesting. Inspiring awe and reverence— appreciation for the confidence displayed here. We lost ourselves in ooos and ahs and surprises here or there for a little while.

As the show neared the end, we had no idea of the finale planned. From the left corner of the stage, the falconer stood still for dramatic effect, holding his arm over a blanket, poised to release. The audience felt a strong wind rise up and blow across our faces from a shock of white plumage, so many wings flapping. My hand found its way to my mouth, stifling a deep gasp.

A large flock of white doves flew diagonally over the gaping faces in the audience and circled back to dock in front of us, looking directly into our eyes. The scene was breathtaking. Magnificent. Surely unexpected at a "Birds of Prey" show.

I would love to see such an explosion of white wings today.

28

"I have called you by name; you are mine"

I cannot rearrange the plot twist here like I could in a work of fiction. These characters are not simply realistic depictions that resonate with the invested reader. I cannot orchestrate a tidy conclusion, tie it up nicely and close the book, for my story is real. It has at its core a story arc that I do not know how to resolve. Who will do an effective character analysis? Who really *is* this main character?

I carry around a stainless-steel water bottle decorated with some artwork that says, "I am who You say I am. Isaiah 43:1." I love the sentiment—My Creator decides who I am, not my peers or my culture, or my past. The verse in reference does not exactly say these words—almost as if it is a misquote, but it is not really if you examine it closely. The message is that the One who created me, dare I reiterate—created my DNA, literally formed me, called me by name. Okay, the verse is talking about Jacob, but I think I can stretch my faith to think of myself as *adopted* into that original family who calls on the God of Abraham, Isaac and Jacob. The Most High God knows my name. Knows who I am. Even if I do not. He is the writer of the story.

I have felt many times that I would like to speak to my mom now about this whole situation, but I wonder what I would say. "You should not have done this. You should not have kept it hidden from me." But, in a way, I am glad I did not know when I was young. And I guess I must admit that I am weirdly glad it happened at all because, obviously, I would not even exist if the specific spermatozoa had not fertilized that particular ovum. Neither would my children. Or their children. This can become a never-ending, underground tunnel, and I must come up for air. I *was* born. My children are here now, so if some magic like we see in movies could offer me a chance to go back and stop this whole fiasco from happening, I would have to decline. The changes in history would be too drastic. That's sobering. I would not want to be someone else with other children. I only want the ones I have, of course. The unique, quirky ones who can cause me to stop breathing from laughing too hard. The utterly precious ones. They are a hundred percent mine. My genetic descendants. And who knows what they will become or produce—how they will contribute to this world. Their purpose. And knowing the truth now about our genetics does not diminish those relationships at all. Not in the same way the truth seems to reduce the other connections. But even those—what made me an aunt to my niece and nephew, for instance, is our relationship. Our experiences together. I watched them grow up and spent time loving them as best I could, any chance I got. It is not our shared genetic material alone that connects us. I think I am who I always was; at least I tell myself that I am still me. Jagged scars and all. I keep reiterating that mantra as if I can make it feel as true as it is.

I am curious to know about this man named Jan. I would like to know if he knew of my existence all along. Did my mom forbid him from seeing me? That would not even bother me so much if that were the case—trying to fit him in somewhere back in my childhood would have caused confusion to infect everything. Or, on the other hand, did Jan just simply reject me? Did he refuse to believe I came from him and, therefore, choose not to see me? Again, I have no anger about the possibilities, just curiosity.

My dad stood in his place, and so the feeling of rejection never contaminated my psyche. I am me partly because of my dad. I do wish, however, that I could interview Jan without his knowing who I was, like a journalist gathering snippets for a story, but he is long past his time living on this earth, a lost suspect, so I will never get the opportunity to jot down key quotes or other notes to paper. And the new-found relatives are also pretty tight-lipped. I reached out a couple of times despite Maria's reluctance to tell her siblings, but none of the relatives responded to my inquiries, even though I kept them quite generic so as not to scare anyone off with something extreme like, "Hey I found out I am your half-sister." I may have been using discontinued emails—who knows? Alas, I am tasked with keeping this knowledge wrapped up and gathering dust, like some valuable archeological find that will never be shared or put on display anywhere. No one will ever benefit from seeing this unearthed treasure from an accidental dig. The suppression of my find *does* take a physical toll, though, and I am unsure if it is really worth the constant pressure of holding the secret captive. . . until I imagine telling my family, that is. Once I picture the hurt or disappointment in their reactions, or the disintegrating familial threads, I continue my effort of concealing. I resist the urge to step out and walk on that water above.

Part IV

You whose scarred hands that begged for holding

Held me

Remain almost tangible

Souls engrave a mark almost legible

29

My Father Gave Me Life

They say people only have a couple, if any, vague memories from ages one to five. I have two vivid memories from when I still slept in a crib. One is a nightmare of an orange and black striped spider crawling up the wall, visible through the blonde rungs of my crib gate. As I opened my eyes and let out a blood curdling shriek, the spider image slowly dissolved as it somersaulted over and over, end over end, falling. . . down and away from my view. That's how I know today that it was a dream and not an actual spider. But at the time, I remember screaming and crying out for my mommy and daddy. Norm picked me up out of the crib, flicked on the light switch and walked me around the room while he investigated the room's corners and the rug under my crib, gently assuring me that there was no spider. I remember his soothing voice,

"See? No spider. You're safe. I promise." Somehow, I went back to sleep. Yet the memory of that spider has remained as a photograph in my mind. And I wonder from where it originated. The frightening image coexists with the fact that my dad's tender assurance calmed me.

Trauma has taken on somewhat of a modern and commonplace meaning these days, and therapists commonly draw out moments from the past that may have been sitting quietly in the back corners of one's mind where the lights have burnt out long ago. Perhaps later in life, maybe in some stealthy efforts, those moments stir and creep out to disrupt the adult's present circumstances, causing her to seek some clarity about her past that she thought was peacefully asleep. Said adult might have forgotten about the trauma or might just choose to see it as some unidentifiable piece of garbage floating among the collecting detritus of human brains. I joke that if I went to therapy, the doctor would have a field day uncovering possible guilty culprits for my quirks or anxieties.

For instance, here's one. In the days of old-fashioned furnaces with a standing pilot light, the gas burned constantly instead of electronically igniting only when needed to force heat through the ducts. When I was under five years old, my family experienced a near-tragic event. The memories of being awakened in the middle of the night to fear and chaos play through my mind like a choppy 8mm film. My sister woke up at 3am with a sudden need to vomit but, thankfully, woke my parents first. The house was unusually cold as my parents stirred, and my dad immediately realized that the furnace's pilot light went out and carbon monoxide was seeping through the house. "Get everybody out," he screamed. "I'll get Michelle." As my mom ran down the hall toward the front door, she collapsed. My dad grabbed me from the crib as I puked all over the front of my pajamas. He set me on the front lawn with my brother and sister and ran back inside to half carry, half drag my mom outside while she slowly regained consciousness. My mom thereafter always recounted the story, describing her thoughts as she lay unconscious on the hallway floor. She imagined that people stood by surrounding her, looking down and assuming she was already dead. Planning to bury her. And she desperately wanted to tell them she was alive but could not get the words out or move a muscle. At some point, someone called the fire department. Trucks parked in front of our house, and my siblings and I were bustled over to a neighbor's house to sleep the rest of the morning while dad arranged for a new furnace to be installed. We were thankful for my sister feeling sick and actually waking up to tell someone. My parents made no effort to hide the fact that if she had not awakened them, we would have all died in our sleep that night. I would not be here. My children and my grandchildren would not be here. It is not lost on me that my dad carried me to fresh air and gave me life.

My father gave me life in many ways, if not in the traditional way we all know. As my mom always said, he *was* a good provider. He provided a home and food and care, sure. But he also provided a family history. A history that I absorbed as if it were grafted into my cells. I may not have been born with it—that family history was not coded into my DNA as I developed, but I feel as if my blood were transfused with much-needed nutrients that kept me growing. At some point, someone like a computer programmer entered the data, and I picked up the traits of this Italian father in a way similar to a person who lives in a foreign country starts picking up mannerisms and acting like a native. I began gathering bits and pieces of this alternate history to pass down to those after me. My legacy.

One of my dad's home movies shows my family and me as a baby, maybe one and a half years old, on a camping trip in Manistee, Michigan next to the strong streamflow near the river, the water excitingly somersaulting over pebbles and crags, waving as it coursed forward, save the portions my dad captured for me. Mom is filming dad holding me in one arm over the fresh torrent, cupping water into his other hand and then directly into my eager mouth. My siblings are sitting on rocks nearby watching and smiling at their baby sister. Cheering her on. We always chuckled at the look on my babyface as I drank and drank, so enjoying the refreshment. It would seem that I only remember this incident because I have seen the film, and that is partly true. But I do remember the taste of that water, cold and pure. Letting my child drink straight from the river is not something I would ever do today. Too much knowledge of parasites and pollution has forever tainted such an idea. But back then, I only trusted what my parents fed me. And it was unadulterated.

The story of my origins is similar. I took in the water from my parents, microscopic debris included, but the contamination was not enough to make me sick, or so I thought. The harmless young parasites grew over time, and they have made themselves known in recent years. Drinking that cool, refreshing water is only a memory, never to be reenacted. And how to cleanse myself of the pestilence now is no easy task. Sometimes I picture, in a nightmarish vision, being dropped into that current and thrashing around for my dad to rescue me. I can shake myself to a more wakeful state and then still feel his strong arms clutching me out of the water and holding me close. My heartbeat slows, and I rest my head on his shoulder. But I cannot taste that pure water anymore no matter how much I seek such refreshment. I have felt parched and searched to alleviate the dehydration but found only drops here and there that help a little. I realize that nothing will quench the genuine thirst the way it did back when I was a baby taking it from my dad's own hand.

Similarly, driving through my old neighborhood, I notice the metal, safety bars on most of the front doors and windows. Dandelions dotting the lawns and high grass around the trees by the street. As I survey the fields behind my childhood home, I lament a great loss. The pathways are overgrown with trees and brush that no one has pruned over the years, so one can no longer get to the deeper parts of the woods. I try to show my daughters what a wonderland I grew up in, but it does not present that way now. The area looks dark and daunting and is probably not safe anymore anyway. People likely do not let their children play in a forest unattended these days, especially near the city. Sometimes I long to walk those very fields and see if I can find my old fire pit or the boulders left from ancient times, and maybe sit at the make-believe theater and clap for a private fairy performance, if they're still dancing, that is. But my woods, as it was, exists only in my dreams now. Curiously, every time I do dream of home, even if I am an adult in my dream, it is *this* home I imagine. My childhood house has remained my

169

house in visions, but I really must stay away from it physically these days and be content to visit it only in my mind. I prefer my mind's view over reality anyway. The one where children freely roam the trails, grounding themselves with the earth beneath their bare feet. Building forts and exercising imagination, creating stories that will last a lifetime. As if those days are recorded on an old cassette tape, and I can rewind and hit play once more, I can hear the laughter and the hooting in little cartoonish voices. The wooded land that was my playground molded me—nurtured me. I think that place was a gift from my dad. It was beautiful then, even if today it is nothing but a tangled mess. Although the chink producing a gap between what was and what is keeps getting wider, I wish to rest with these visions of childhood untainted by reality; *that* is who I was. That *is* my reality despite what is true today.

30

My Father's Hands

I was so afraid in the weeks following his death that others would forget what a catastrophic event I had just experienced losing my dad. I used to think the rituals of viewing a dead body in a parlor were antiquated. Sort of morbid to wear black or even a black armband for a period after a loved one passed as was the custom a generation or so ago. As an opinionated teenager, I would claim that the person's soul was no longer in that body so no need to stare at it and go through these ceremonial motions of lengthy processions and burials.

But when Norm passed, my views shifted. My sister and brother allowed me to arrange the details of the funeral. I suddenly wanted all of the traditions. Down to the roses in each of our hands to throw on the coffin as it was lowered into the ground by each of my dad's nephews fulfilling the great honor of being his pall bearers. Down to the black dress I wore, and the black arm band I wish were still the protocol to signify to the world that one was in mourning. Stopping into a CVS or a grocery store in weeks following, a simple, "How are you doing today" from the cashier could trigger tears or an inability to catch my breath. I wanted to say, "I just lost my dad, so not very well, thank you." I wanted to say, "Look at my arm band. How dare you ask how I am doing?" I then realized what those rituals from the past were for. They were a silent reminder to be gentle with the mourner. Do not talk about frivolous things. Do not bring up negative past events. Just show a little understanding that this person standing in front of you, trying to get on with life, maybe buying some milk and bread for the family, needs to learn to navigate this new life. How to move forward when only the past occupies their mind for a time.

We heard such nice things at my dad's funeral. But one guest that day casually remarked, not knowing that I overheard, that it is strange how people elevate the dead after they are gone. Everyone disregards the very real, perhaps negative, events or personality traits of the honoree. Instead, the eulogy commemorates the person's character as if he were *only* good. Not truly human then like the rest of us. I didn't like hearing this, especially at the memorial service no less. Why would I want to highlight drunken parties or affairs and unload all of our dirty laundry in front of guests sad to see my father go?

Some people even say they do not want a funeral at all. They direct people on what to do after their own death as if it is *their* call. And family members feel they must honor that decision. I contend that funerals are for the living. A time when they need to reflect on the life, the legacy, the future that will be forever different without that person. And most people need the closure anyway. At my dad's funeral, I just wanted to lift him up. Send him off with sort of a thank-you for molding my life and touching the lives of so many others. Two of my dad's cousins who traveled from southern Ohio to Michigan for his memorial service were delayed on the way. They finally arrived at the church just when the service concluded and the casket had been closed for the short trip to the gravesite for burial. All the guests were milling about, getting to their cars for the procession when the pastor and the funeral director noticed the cousins' dismay because they missed seeing Norm's body and saying goodbye face-to-face. Kindly, the director invited this couple to the casket with no one else in the sanctuary and opened it back up so they could spend a few minutes alone with their cousin, one last time. I watched from the foyer as they bent over the coffin talking to my dad, smiling and touching his cool, folded hands with familiarity and comfort. They couldn't keep back their words of thanks at this little gesture meant to help them put my dad to rest.

At the wake, my dad's first, so his eldest, nephew made a point to tell me what my dad meant to him. He was quite a bit older than me and lived out of state, so I never really knew this cousin as well as some of the others. He had grown up with both my dad's sister Celia and my dad doting on him, but in completely different ways. Celia was always interested in literature, a personality trait I assumed I inherited since I majored in English lit and became a teacher, just like my aunt. Aunt Celia took her nephew, Don, to libraries and museums, instilling in him an appreciation for art and culture. Travel to Europe, she also encouraged to widen his horizons.

Uncle Norm, however, took Don to the woods. He taught him survival skills and a love of nature's organic beauty. How good for the soul is feeling that mud squish right between your toes. Celia was college educated. Norm was not. Norm showed Don his roots—the hills of West Virginia. Swimming in the waterfalls that came rushing down those mountains, near Blackwater Falls. Don's daughter sings John Denver's *Country Roads* at every family member's funeral.

Don really wanted me to know that he was well-rounded as a man because of having both his aunt's influence and my dad's. Unexpectedly, I noticed that Don's hands were exactly like my dad's, shape and texture. I couldn't help but stare as he talked. He wanted me to know that while both sides of his upbringing were important, my dad was a truly significant role model for him. With tears just threatening to overflow, Don looked in my eyes.

"Your dad gave me so much, Michelle. I don't know if you could ever understand just how influential he was. There is absolutely no way Uncle Norm will ever be forgotten. In a very real and physical sense, he is part of me." I asked him if he minded me just sitting with him and holding his hand for a while to feel that closeness and kinship that had trickled down several different connected pipelines to somehow form such a similarity as these hands.

Genetics are funny that way.

31

"For you created my inmost being; you knit me together in my mother's womb"

Looking back at parts of childhood in my family has always been somewhat, must I again describe it with that overused word that has lost much of its punch these days, *traumatic* enough before the question of paternity ever sidled up close. Like walking through a cave, I would feel minor quakes shaking some of the boulders loose, making small piles of rubble behind me. But I had always managed to go forward, already having stayed just ahead of those heaps that I only noticed the wreckage if I craned my neck to view the past. I could always see the warm light in the future cheering me on. Now, I have come to a spot where so many stalagmites are blocking that light. I can feel a temperature change, some warmth beckoning me with a steady hand, but some of these spikes are thicker than others and they are difficult to get around. It's a challenging game of wit and strength to complete this obstacle course.

These new relatives are so much older than I that as each year passes without my meeting any of them, the game seems hardly worth the prize, and I am getting weary. I could just exit this cave and forfeit, pretending I never learned a different past. I could stay in a state of denial, continuing my relationships with my original siblings and cousins while the truth slinks around us like a ghost only I can see. People tell me that is not a healthy path. I have been playing a dangerous game as sometimes ghosts have a mind to appear in solid form to those with a keen perception, and I might not be able to keep mine quiet forever. What will I say to my aunt Celia if all of this comes out? Also, the responsibility is mine alone to keep my mom's reputation intact since I am the only one who knows this muffled ghost. And I can picture metaphorically being whisked away from my aunt by some powerful vacuum once she realizes I am no relation to her by blood. Of course, people who love you do not let your relationship disintegrate so easily, but can they really control such a force that might control their feelings unwittingly?

I never struggled with that somewhat typical teenage identity crisis growing up. I felt rather secure in who I was back then—even as my role in the alcoholic family started taking shape. I was the fixer. Encourage everyone to take their own responsibilities. Realize that your parents' addictions are not your fault. Neither are their mistakes. Relationships are more important than circumstances. Forgiveness is more for yourself than for the offenders. Perhaps this is all common knowledge these days as we see little memes pop up on Instagram with this backyard psychology, but when I was coming up, one had to read some helpful literature or sit under a strong and wise mentor to come out of addicted families virtually unscathed. I somehow managed that. I learned that my parents did the best they could with what few tools they had.

Mom probably never felt loved and cherished by her father as a child, and she grew up trying to fill some cavern in her soul with the love of a man. Dad was busy with his work travel and his hobbies and didn't really notice that his wife was so unfulfilled. They sat under no religious teaching, nor did they attend marriage conferences that have become more popular in my generation and might have provided some useful skills or insight. And no one went to therapy in those days, it seemed. Perhaps the one effort exerted was a weekend "Marriage Encounter" where mom and dad supposedly wrote letters to each other expressing either love or forgiveness. After returning, they may have simply placed the idea of divorce on the back burner for a while. But they had no older, wiser married couples in their lives to model the continuing work a loving or lasting marriage must entail. They never read something like, *The Five Love Languages: The Secret to Love That Lasts*, for that book did not become popular until the 1990s. Yet they did not fully tear apart after all. Most of what they took from one another, they finally gave back to each other and built something new, a few missing pieces notwithstanding, and stayed the course until the end. In some display of dramatic irony, I felt the love my mother never could from the man she thought deficient, and I received nothing but the initial fertilization that began my life from the man with whom my mother sought fulfillment. It seems that maybe I am still me—who I always was. It is my mother who is someone different. Someone I must have never fully known.

Today was not the first time this has happened. I awoke in the early hours of the morning with the same dream fluttering atop my eyelids, urging them to open before the situation settled back as fiction rather than the reality it pretended to be. In truth, we were heading to my granddaughter's ballet performance in the week ahead, and my mom always enjoyed dance. She was a faithful supporter of her own grandchildren's recitals in the past, even in her last week of life when we broke her out of the hospital to watch my daughter's spring recital, even as she nodded off several times desperately trying in her weakness to hold her gaze on the stage. As I woke, still in darkness, I felt this overwhelming urge to get up and phone my mother before letting any more time pass and invite her to go with us to the theater. The illusory feeling remaining, as if she had been alive all these years and I had just neglected to call. The guilt seeped in and threatened to drown me for a few seconds, keeping the truth hidden. Slowly, the curtain was drawn open as the dream disintegrated and the realization took form in front of me. She was not here. I had not forgotten to invite her. She would not be joining us.

That urge to call mom will never leave us. My mom told me that many years ago about her own mother. Every time something good or exciting happens, or the opposite— something heart wrenching happens, the first impulse is to pick up the phone and talk to my mom. I want to tell her the funny things about my grandchildren because I know she, of all people, will appreciate them and disburse that valuable laughter all around us. In fact, some of their little quirks remind me of her. She indeed passed down some precious traits. And she will agree with everyone who claims that the littlest girl looks just like me. But she will be the one trusted most to confirm this observation with authority since she was there as I toddled along and grew into adulthood. Even in my wakefulness, I feel compelled to reach for the phone.

I have said I wish I did not know the truth about my past and that I wish I could return to that state of not-knowing, but, of course, we cannot repackage this story that has been splayed out before me. The box is damaged, and nothing fits back in it properly. Now, the question is what to do with this knowledge. Where are the instructions on how to assemble all the pieces to make me a whole person again with a new identity? I never was into jigsaw puzzles or building model cars, like my brother was, and I do not feel smart enough to construct something out of such a mess of pieces. And besides, the structure of DNA is infinitely more complicated than a puzzle. That's why I have never had trouble believing the scripture that declares The God of the Universe formed my innermost being in the womb. Only an omnipotent God could put a complex being together in all its intricate details. According to *The National Library of Medicine*, the nucleus of each human cell, which is only about six micrometers in diameter, contains about two meters of DNA. To picture this seemingly impossible task, understand that a micrometer is equal to about one millionth of a meter. One textbook called, *The Molecular Biology of the Cell*, describes the complexity as packing twenty-four miles of fine thread into a tennis ball. For *every* cell. How do such long strands fit inside such a small space and play out in the formation of a human being just so?

Truth is light. For years, I have been feeling like the opposite is true. I have felt that the time before my mom told me her secret was my light. I lived and grew up as Michelle, with my place card situated right where it was supposed to be: at the dining table between mom and dad. We drew up added chairs for my sister's children, my brother's, and my children later, and we all sat together for a while, connected by a good meal and the strands that intertwine among family, like ivy on solid structures, even if those structures had some flaws hidden underneath the foliage. Stepping out of that dining room to the truth has felt like stepping *into* darkness. The DNA test seemed to have turned off the light.

But something is flickering in the recesses of my mind, like a spark of electricity purposely trying to trip this memory, the remembrance of who I am. And the recollection, and profound significance, of my dad's last days on earth.

Part V

Memories, Visions, Dreams

My grasping

Inhabitation

Salvation

Hearts return from whence they came

Yet still remain

32

Rescue

Back many years now, the day my dad's appendix ruptured, my kids were running a sac race under the unforgiving July sun at our annual Summer Family Camp. Beads of sweat mixed with a little dust collected from our cheerleading event in front of the volleyball pit nearby and etched dirty lines down the sides of my face.

We'll hit the pool next, I thought, trying to convince myself that this wasn't so bad. I could certainly suffer through another few minutes. The girls were having fun after all. Over the loudspeaker, usually used for announcements about schedule changes or contest results, I heard my name and the request to come in for an important phone call. All members of my immediate family were here, safe with me. No one calls me at camp. I had purposely abandoned my mobile phone in the car without any worry.

Thoughts swam in all directions as I jogged over to the office and a short, portly woman ushered me into the back room with a concerned expression on her face. I heard the raucous rattling of air conditioning from the old window unit announcing its effort to cover this small space but felt no cooling relief.

As soon as I heard my mom's voice, I knew. She struggled through a couple of mostly nonsensical words, her voice cracking.

"It's about your dad."

"Do you really think this is it, mom?" A seemingly interminable pause followed. "Is it that serious? We need to come home?"

My husband and I gathered our scattered belongings in a hurry, left the children with another family and hopped in the car holding printed directions to this little hospital in the middle of nowhere where my dad lay in a coma, intubated, and connected to a dialysis machine that we found out later was so rickety it couldn't function for the twenty-four hours a day needed.

Almost as clearly as an angel brought Saint Joseph extremely important directions in a dream, some messenger engendered in my mind the thought of this small-town pastor we met years before. I had heard this man speak once at a funeral and didn't even remember his name. His words were a balm to the elderly mourners those years prior, and something comforting radiated from his face the few times I passed him in the local grocery while visiting my parents in the rural setting where they chose to spend their senior years.

In fact, my mom said when she caught his eye a few times in town, he seemed to look right into her soul as if he *knew* her. She would not dare step foot in his little 19th century church, what with my dad's opposition to anything faith-based standing in her way, but she had wanted to a couple of times.

Calling him seemed a reasonable endeavor since my husband and I were on the three-hour drive that would take us to my dad's bedside, likely in time for his death. Desperation took over. I needed someone for my mom while she waited for us to arrive. She hadn't the stamina, nor the faith needed in situations like these. Someone should sit with her and offer at least some kind words. And if this was my dad's time to pass, he needed a spiritual presence as well. I called the city clerk for the name of the church and then scrambled to find someone who knew how to put me in touch with the minister, Lloyd Williams.

"Uh, Pastor Lloyd, you don't know me, but my mom is stuck at the hospital witnessing my dad's last hours, and she could use someone to talk to. Would you consider calling her or driving over while we are on our way, still a few hours out?" I paused before adding,

"Oh and by the way, I've got to tell you--they are—um--non-believers—and not your average non-believers. My dad is more like maybe. . . a God-hater. Mom will appreciate the help, but he. . ." I struggled to describe him. "That's another story."

"Of course," he responded. "I'll head over there right now, and don't worry. I've been around people without faith before. I'm quite sure I can handle it." I now imagine his gentle smile that I later came to know.

"Um. . . you might not understand the severity. Religious people make him sick. Yeah, many claim that in front of like-minded friends, but he is the type who may just want to hit you if he wakes up," I explained as an effort of true warning. My dad's reactions to spiritual matters had always evoked strong responses from his otherwise friendly self.

"I'm not asking for Bible reading or prayers at his bedside. I just need someone to lend a shoulder to my mom right now. Hopefully, we will get there in time to say our good-byes to my dad." I said these words without tears, not because I didn't care but because the business of the moment called for action to hold emotion at bay. There would be time for tears later as we watched him leave his life on that table under white sheets and amid plenty of plastic tubing.

"Point taken. I'll be aware." Pastor Lloyd said, trying to dispel my legitimate fears of getting himself hurt if my dad awoke. "I know just who your mom is. I've seen her in the grocery store a few times. She wants to reach out. I can tell," he said, likely signing to his wife that he had to go immediately to the hospital. I'm sure she was used to this behavior, as she later told me she just wrapped up something for him to eat on the run and handed him his keys. It was simply a routine for them to drop everything and aid others.

While my husband drove, I kept rubbing my sweaty palms up and down the texture of my cargo pants thinking about my last words. I had always hoped there would be a meaningful exchange between the two of us, not simply my speaking my hope in an afterlife into the deaf ears of a dying father. *This can't be the end. He never accepted this faith. It's happening too fast.*

When we arrived, a little disheveled, I expected to find my mom sitting with this nice man as he would be consoling her and quietly waiting for her family to take over. Maybe he would be praying or something else very pastor-like. I did not expect to find him conversing with the doctors in the hall right outside of my dad's room where he had spent some time reading Psalms and praying with my dad. The nurses knew Lloyd on a first-name basis, and my mom felt as if he were taking care of everything, from where she would stay that night, to what doctors would be coming to update the family and helping us decide whether or not we should airlift my dad to the more advanced, university hospital sixty miles away. He had comforted my mom, yes, but he also took control in both a gentle and a firm way, a way that none of us could at the time.

The spinning blades flapped a worthy breeze for the few of us standing on the roof of the hospital, my mom, my brother, my husband and me. And Pastor Lloyd too. It had been such a hot day, and we were likely sweating from not only the elements but from the rushed decisions we had to make regarding my dad's care.

Doctors had austerely presented our either/or option: we could leave my dad in this small country hospital and take our chances that his kidneys would bounce back with that old dialysis machine, or we could fly him to the University hospital and up the chances that he might survive this ordeal. Seems an obvious choice, but the trip over to the university cast a shadow of doubt. Would he even make it to the other doctors? But staying here, we knew we had little chance of seeing dad recover from the sepsis taking over.

The decision fell to me, like a test I hadn't studied ahead for. My mom barely functioned at this point after the shock of her day and seeing my dad lay inert, intubated, in a coma. And My brother remained stoic as usual. I have probably only heard a few words from him my whole life. I became my dad's patient advocate. I did not yet know what an important role that is.

Once the staff loaded dad onto the helicopter and we watched the craft lift to the dark sky, all of us grabbed hands.

Prompted by our new pastor friend, we prayed. Before that point, and after, I had *never* witnessed my brother pray. Here we were earnestly grasping each other and pleading for mercy. A chance for our dad to make it through this ordeal. I wanted to talk to my dad one more time. We all did.

At the next hospital, we met a team of eager doctors, a very young Dr. Schmit as their spokesman, maybe younger than myself—the first time I would encounter a doctor younger than me. I was only 33. The team waited with a palpable excitement to get started on this new challenge: bring Norm back to life. Dr. Schmit assured me that he thought he could indeed save my dad. He had a plan. For one, the dialysis machine would work twenty-four hours a day here.

What an invention—a machine that filters the toxins from our body, a giant artificial kidney perfectly matched to the patient, working without protest. Without being old and tired and giving up in defeat from all the poison clogging the system. The machine worked metaphorically as well because it certainly filtered a lot of gunk out of dad's system during his stay.

The four-month sentence my dad experienced, first in ICU, and later, on various floors of the hospital and rehabilitation center, took its toll on those of us not exactly in his prison but within sight of the punishment his body took. It's not easy to watch such atrophy, and while some try to compensate with the fact—*at least it's not physically happening to me*—empathy raises its head, stares you in the face, and invites you to feel as if it were. When one thing was fixed, another broke. Lungs that threatened to never work again gasped at oxygen that raised them from the dead. But then the kidneys still lay lifeless, relying on that upgraded machine at this vanguard hospital to which we gratefully moved him. Once they sputtered to life again, the heart expressed a few warnings. Muscles refused to repair. Intestines were sluggish. The damaged pancreas caused drastic sugar spikes or plummets. It was a game of tear and mend, rip and patch as doctors seemed to be practicing on a material that was not as resilient as they believed it to be.

Pastor Lloyd trekked out to the hospital, an hour away from his house, every day for months and spent time over the bedside of my dad--the inactive geriatric patient. My very real warnings of my father's inevitable reaction if and when he awoke from this state to find such a devout man invading his personal space bounced off Lloyd and returned with a chuckle. How could he know the horrible things my dad had said in the past about religious nuts. I could never repeat such colorful language to which I had become accustomed.

As Lloyd read passages from scripture describing the metaphorical mansions beyond this world promised in John, Chapter 14, or relating the mercy bestowed upon us from The Creator, the One who carefully knit us together in our mother's womb, none of us imagined how these words penetrated my father's stupor and mingled with both sane images and nightmarish visions of seemingly three-dimensional demons, manifested as ghouls chasing him down some dark path to suck the air out of him, just like the dementors JK Rowling portrays.

Sure enough, when my dad regained consciousness, he strained to reach Lloyd, and with his arms still affixed to the side rails and his speech muffled by the plastic tubes down his throat, his agitation intimated violence. When the nurse untied him, despite my protests, Lloyd bent down for the embrace he was confident my dad meant to share.

The two men had bonded across realms and shared commonalities the rest of us didn't yet know. They hugged, and my dad caught my eye. He couldn't speak for the thick tubes, but he clearly gestured a thank-you to me for arranging this *helper* that led him out of the literal darkness of his coma, both medically and spiritually. We had been to the valley of the shadow of death and found a way up the side of the mountain.

For the first time in fifty plus years, other than for a wedding or funeral, my dad expressed a desire to attend church one Sunday to hear Lloyd preach. It would be no easy task to obtain a day pass from the rehab center to drive my dad the hour trip with an oxygen tank stowed in the trunk, a borrowed wheelchair, a plank to slide his dead weight in and out of the car, and a bag of various medicines should we need something, like an emergency insulin shot. Though I didn't feel qualified, I felt determined to accommodate my dad's surprising request. We joked about the walls falling down on us in protest when he entered the building.

But the walls stood firm, seemingly held up by outstretched arms of singers offering praise.

Take my hands, Lord, and let them move
At the impulse of Thy love.
Take my life, Lord . . .

True worship, I'm told, is in honoring and serving people, not just singing spiritual songs in a church building. In the months prior to this visit, members of Lloyd's congregation who had never met my dad wrote letters and sent cards, hundreds of them, with heart-felt encouragement. Weeping at such unfamiliar behavior, my dad questioned:

Why would people do this when they don't even know me? I'm nobody to them, and they don't realize what kind of a person I really am.

They prayed strength and light into him, healing him from deep within. These men and women served in such a way that they had somehow tied a cord from themselves to my dad and had been gently pulling him toward them over these months of recuperation. When we pushed the wheelchair in through the back entrance of the church, people began turning around mid-song as if they felt this new presence behind them. Some hugged my dad or patted him on the back prior to the start of the sermon as if he were a regular attendee and they were all friends. We felt their physical touch in a handshake or an embrace, confirming that they were actually real people and not angelic beings fabricated in our minds as we lay dreaming.

Do people like this truly exist in little havens around the world? People who care about one sick, bitter, old man in need of someone's hands to hold onto a lifeless heart and squeeze until it begins beating again? As we wheeled him to an open spot, everyone stood clapping, an ovation for a man who *was* dead and unknown but was now alive and very much known. Lloyd's preaching that day was fueled by something otherworldly, the Spirit itself. We felt fed and full.

On the drive back to the rehab center, his temporary home for the last several months, my dad expressed how pleased he was with his own progress. Everything was coming together for him. His body was making its way back to independent functionality, and, most of all, his spirit was renewed, ready for graduation day from his long stay in the hospital. He smiled at the reality that he would be coming home that very week after four months in acute care. The doctors hadn't really expected this level of recovery of his aged and abused body; we knew we experienced a true-blue miracle.

"I'm feeling sort of like we cheated death back there," dad said, taking a long look at me driving. "I was meant to go back in July, wasn't I?" Pointing up to the sky, he acknowledged, "He healed me for some reason, I know that. I guess I just wasn't ready for the end when I kind of slammed up against it, ya know?"

Returning well after dark to a couple of nurses' aides, we sheepishly relinquished my dad into their capable hands. What did it matter now if we were late? He was going to be released in a couple of days anyway. Marietta, a tall, capable, beautiful woman of color who had taken a liking to my dad, scolded us with mock seriousness as she got Norm into a nightshirt and effortlessly lifted him from the wheelchair into bed, kissing him on the forehead as she did so.

"Why'd you stay out so late?" She took his hands into hers and got right up in his face. "You know it's up to me to take care of you, and I was missing you tonight!" My dad held onto her hands a little longer than necessary and peered back into her eyes with a little smile.

"I missed you too. You take such good care of me. . . like my own daughter. You hear? Like my own daughter." He pulled me close too and kissed me goodnight. In the embrace, I inhaled the familiar scent. Soapy and outdoorsy. A contrast to the medicinal smells of the rehab center.

"I love you, honey. Thanks for taking me out today." Those were his last words to me. His heart stopped the next morning, and despite thirty minutes of resuscitative efforts, it refused to start up again.

33

Trust

Sometimes when I seek answers or help from The Creator of the universe, I feel guilty. Small and insignificant. I obviously have a little angst over my past. Over the revelation that I am not my father's biological daughter. I missed out on meeting blood relatives and cultivating relationships with these genetically linked connections. But considering the state of the world, this issue pales. Whenever I start to pray for myself, images of starving or abused children shoot across the canvas in my line of vision like arrows hissing by, dangerously close. How can I pray for my struggle when someone nearby is losing a child or going through the pain of cancer? Sunday school teachers have taught that God is sovereign, above all, involved in everyone's lives simultaneously.

How can that be? How can He care about someone's cursory prayer for "safe travels," for example, when another mother has watched her child suffer and die in a devasting car accident? Sometimes I wake in the middle of the night with one of my frequent stomachaches and start to pray for healing and rescue. Then I think of someone asking for the healing of a terminal disease, and I feel ashamed. How can God listen to both prayers at the same time and not shake His head or roll His eyes?

I suppose I am attributing human emotions and capacities to the Divine here. Just because I do not understand this capability does not mean it is not possible.

But I would *like* to understand it. I realize I have trust issues. It does not take a psychology degree to determine where these trust issues come from, but I really did not identify them until their presence unexpectantly smacked me right in the face one summer.

Family Camp, the same place we spent every 4th of July when our children were growing up and the same place we were when we got the news of my dad's brush with death, provides numerous recreational activities, and some learning opportunities too. The High Ropes Course, meant to deliver thrilling fun, also teaches you some things about yourself. The multiple safety measures should make the participant feel secure. Back many summers ago, this was an exciting activity to try with my teenaged kids. I had no fear when the coach hooked me up to the very strong cord, harness, and carabiner clip.

Climbing the telephone pole to the first challenge on the course, a swinging rope bridge, took a little of my courage away, and I could feel some tightening in my airways, probably causing a lack of oxygen and, therefore, some dizziness. But this was nothing I could not calm down with a couple of slow, deep breaths. The fear of heights had never plagued me before. The course, though, seems set up to trick your mind. Walking across the bridge just feels wrong. Swinging back and forth high above a solid ground is foreign to the senses no matter how much confidence you possess. Yes, the cable will save your life, but the body will still feel the fall. And the images entering the brain keep shouting-- stop this dangerous task. You are not meant to walk this high above ground. Several challenges increase the fight or flight reaction common to us all at certain times. Climbing yet higher and hopping from one small, wooden step to another really causes you to face the possibility of death. But I could laugh through my new-found trepidation to the end of the course, feeling like I conquered such a foe and showed my daughters how to step into fear and control it. Good life lesson, I thought. Until I got to the last task.

I had to stand in the "bird's nest" loft, extremely high above the ground, and let the staffer hold onto the back of my harness until he was ready to shove me off to a zip line slanted down to the ground in a free fall. Perhaps the image of my brother falling manifested in front of my mind's eye. Waiting for this young man to make the decision of when to let go was too much for me. I kept needing to restart.

"Wait. Let me get situated again," I'd say, stalling for time. I could not let this young man have total control and push me off the tower. To give up at this point means-- instead of taking the adventurous ride ziplining to the ground, you can climb down another, safer, way. In full control of yourself.

With a little embarrassment showing on my face, I chose to take the easy way down, realizing that I could not trust my exit to another person. And that's when I owned up to this trust issue that had taken root long ago and slowly grew in strength over the years. I never trust others to make decisions for me. I do not trust that people have my best interest in mind and can always handle one situation or another in the most effective way possible. I have a hard time trusting that God desires to heal me or work things out for good when He has a million other, bigger, things to address. I just cannot wrap my head around the idea that He can be engaged with millions of people at the same time.

But I sure hope He can, and I keep asking for help even when I have trouble trusting. I try to go back to that boat in the middle of the storm and let Him do His thing.

Lately, I have tried my hands, or really my feet, at a barre class at the gym. I have never been a ballerina, so the exercises are all new to me, but people tell me the stretching movements build a sense of balance and strength, and this teacher is a physical therapist, so I figure I would do best learning from her. And I have found it easy enough to avoid looking like an idiot when the firmly attached bar acts as the perfect crutch. I grab onto it often and straighten myself out from an awkward contortion too far backward. Our coach keeps the room dimly lit, and I like to lose the tether to my schedule and my cell phone in the pleasant music pulsing through the speakers. When the leader directs us to place our feet in something like fifth position, most of us in the studio are flexible enough, even though we are all of a certain age in the class I choose to attend. All of us likely trying to keep the aging process hovering near graceful.

"Hold your feet close together, closing the gap," she instructs. "Stand tall. Stretch your arms up high. Zip in that core and breathe deep." Inhale. Feel strong, I think.

"Now let go of the bar." No problem. I can balance just fine.

"Now close your eyes. Hold this position." Again, my trust issues do a little jig around me and yank me right down. Off balance. The mind plays tricks, and holding still and straight becomes nearly impossible.

Many of us rely on our crutches and reach out to something steady. We learn how much easier it is to stand when we simply open our eyes. We realize that we need a full view of the room. Perspective. We need to see that we are standing on the same solid ground we were before closing our eyes.

"Open them, look around, and try again." Keep practicing and soon, we will be able to stand steady whether in light or in darkness. Keep practicing. Keep practicing. Eventually, I will stop wobbling so much.

To relax and escape the world sometimes, one of my favorite pastimes these days is to take a leisurely drive to Island Lake and float out on the still waters. My husband does not enjoy that activity as much as I do, but he will accompany me for at least the drive. I leave him sitting on the shore in a fold-up lounge chair with a book in his lap. And I tote my dollar store raft out toward the horizon.

I like to lie on my belly and get out among the tall reeds and face the far side of the lake, looking at the trees on the banks and listening to the ducks and the birds that surround me. I can grasp that same feeling I experienced way back in childhood floating along the river in my woods. Sometimes a school of minnows flit under my hands hanging in the water. Although it's not advisable these days like it was in my childhood, I like to have a little oil on my skin to draw in the sun's rays, welcoming a golden tint.

On this particularly bright day, with the sun directly above dotting a cloudless, sapphire sky, I fall half asleep with my head propped on my folded arms. Here the water and oil have formed hundreds of droplets on my browning shoulders and forearms. I am jolted by an epiphany.

In each tiny droplet, I see a perfect, round reflection of the sun. From that one giant source of fire above, hundreds of little light globes shine forth as individual representations. I can't really explain the physics of this phenomenon, something about refraction I think, but the message isn't lost on me.

34

Redemption

The very evening of the day I read my ancestry results, my daughter, Emily, and her husband were visiting, and we were sitting at the dining table playing a game of dominoes. I was quieter than usual, contemplating the ramifications of what I had just learned. I had never mentioned my mom's infidelity or suspicion of paternity to my daughters. They did not know that I wavered constantly between testing to confirm or letting the question in my heart go unanswered forever. They had never heard that coiled dragon hissing in all of their years, and, obviously, did not know what it took for me to tame it for so long.

While studying her tiles, Em casually piped up with a statement that knocked the wind out of me:

"I think I'm gonna do that DNA testing. Just for fun. I want to see what percentage of everything I am. People are always asking my ethnicity, ya know? Remember those people at work—'What *are* you?'" they always ask. Draw out the "are" as Emily's features are defined but curious. We had always laughed at how some people find such a question offensive, but we know that most people are simply intrigued by her somewhat exotic look and just wonder where she comes from. She has a beautiful shade of olive skin, black hair, and large, almond shaped eyes—greenish blue, like mine. She certainly looks Mediterranean, but her dad *is* a cocktail of Middle Eastern, Mexican and European, so all of those traits could well have bled into her composition. Our eldest daughter, Kate, in stark contrast, has smooth, very fair skin, sun kissed, blond hair and perfectly sky-blue eyes. The two girls have no similar physical characteristics. Many times, in their childhood, when I would cart my children through the grocery store or Target, strangers would feel free to butt in with comments or questions.

"Those girls are not both yours, are they?" Eye roll. "These two can't be sisters, right?" Annoyance filled up like a gas tank, and I gained enough fuel to answer people just to give a little shock:

"Yes, they are both mine, and fortunately for me, they have the same father too. Phew!" I don't know how genes work, but they must have flowed into my two daughters through different passageways.

Excusing myself from our game of dominoes rather abruptly raised some eyebrows. I got myself to the bathroom upstairs and spent a moment with my head over the toilet, dry heaving. Tears welled in my eyes even as I flushed them with cold water, trying to cool the redness down and make my face look unaffected. Knowing what possibility existed, I had grown adept at this concealment of late, but I had just faced the steel hard truth that morning. I had not practiced enough, and I did not expect my daughter to bring up the subject that same day. I took a few deep breaths, in and out, in and out, and I returned to the table. Emily knows her mother. She knew something was wrong, but no way existed for me to tell her at that moment. She asked, but I just rambled on about how I heard some people find out unexpected things and regret doing these DNA tests.

"Are you trying to tell me something? Mom? Dad? Spit it out. Is there a secret here? Are you my real parents?" Nervous chuckles. "Is Kate my biological sister? I can handle it. Go ahead. Tell me." More prodding.

I must have appeased her with some sort of promise to talk to her in more detail at another time, but

"Yes. You are our daughter, a hundred percent genetic, as is your sister. I will not lie to you about anything, but let's table the discussion of DNA testing for another time. I just have some strong feelings about it. Obviously." This does it for a few months and allows me time to figure out how to release this beast only for a short day pass to tell my daughters and then bind him back up again so no one else hears his story. Everyone knows once a secret gets let out for a few people, it gains strength, and it is that much more difficult to reign it back in, hold it down and keep it muffled. Especially if you ask others to help you when they do not have the same incentive you do for keeping the prisoner locked away.

About twelve weeks later, I clicked open a call from Emily.

"Who the hell's Polish?" She chuckled as my stomach dropped yet again. She's always been a little abrupt, like my mom. A little Doris in her, we always say. "Did Gramma not know she was Polish? Is this the big secret? Or is one of you adopted? I don't get it."

Long inhale.

"I'd really like to talk about all this in person. It's a perfect example of what we call 'a tangled web.' You are coming back to town for your old roommate's wedding, right? So let's plan to talk about it then. I will answer all your questions." Long exhale.

"It's too long to wait! All my questions? I guess I have no choice."

Em did wait, and the time went quickly for me before just the two of us took the car for a drive one evening and parked.

"What I have to say is big. . . really big. At least for me." As I began, the tears flowed both ways and the ones behind my sinuses choked my words pretty good. I could hardly say that I found out her Grandpa was not my biological dad. I had always cherished Emily's very emotional words she spoke as a child when my dad passed away all those years ago. Her little voice, strong through tears said, "I just don't think I can live the rest of my life without him." Upon *this* news, she cried, but mostly to console me. I managed to choke out some expressions of embarrassment. Some apology for shattering my mother's reputation. Some anguish about not being Italian. Some regret about her grandparents not being the people she thought they were. Changing her whole view of them and perhaps herself. She could tell I was worried about her hearing this news. How does one unpack this revelation and not breathe in the toxic fumes?

"It's okay, mom. I'm so sorry you have to go through this," she says while stroking my shoulder on her side. She pulled herself together much better than I. With a barely audible giggle, she reasoned. "First of all, I don't care at all that I'm not Italian. I never identified with those roots like you did, or maybe even like Kate did. I mean, Kate learned the language to travel to Italy and investigate all that lineage stuff. I'm not into that. I just care because you care. I know this hurts you. And that's what I don't like. For me, it's not a big thing to worry about. I'm just glad I did not find out that you or dad are not my parents. You didn't just spring on me that I am adopted or something." We both laughed a little.

"We have to tell Kate, though. Now. She could tell earlier that something was up, and I don't want to keep her in the dark."

Em and I Facetimed Kate, and Emily did the talking here. In fact, for years after this, I could not talk about the subject without choking up. I could not push the words past that physical barrier in the back of my throat. Kate accepted the news with a quiet disbelief. She suspected, or hoped, that the DNA results were simply a mistake.

"Maybe Grandpa was not as Italian as he thought and just some of the other genes are showing up. Maybe you inherited mostly from your mom instead of your dad. Or maybe the samples got mixed up. It can't be right."

Everyone throws out these possibilities, I have heard, when the truth tears through that green screen of the fake reality constructed a long time ago. I read a story about the common practice of mixing sperm in the fertility clinics of the 1960s. The thought was that the donated sperm, that was perhaps more robust, could help propel the lazier sperm along, unbeknownst to potential fathers providing their own samples. Knowing my parents' involvement in the fertility world of that time period, I might have liked to hold onto this possibility. Perhaps that method of fertilization would be easier to accept. I may have liked to explain my conception this way, and mom's reputation could have remained intact, a sturdier structure for her children and grandchildren to remember.

Yet I have known since early childhood that I was a surprise baby anyway, not helped along at the clinic. And what Kate would eventually learn was that I not only read my genetic results that were different from what I expected, or hoped, but I had also met a half-sister and learned all about several other family members. Even though I have found no similarities among these new relatives, they are, indeed, the descendants of the very man with whom my mother had a long-term relationship. The DNA site could not have coincidentally connected all the dots and led us to that precise divulgence.

Kate still does not like to talk about the subject, and in her heart, has tucked the knowledge away as possibly mistaken, in a sweetly content, ignorance-is-bliss sort of way. She likely wishes I never told her. While Emily has no problem with the idea of telling our extended family and friends, Kate helps me keep the secret all wrapped up neatly.

We never do let the story go past our immediate family and only one or two of my close friends from childhood. Not even my siblings have touched this nerve in the years since I felt the severed cords. I seemed to have trained professionally in the art of concealment, but I am getting too old for the sport and starting to slip a little.

I had always prayed and hoped I would get to see my dad's conversion, but I never fully trusted, and I never dreamed the event would be so monumental. I thought maybe my dad might shamefacedly admit that he was a sinner and needed a savior and, right before his death, he might quietly ask for forgiveness, ensuring his entrance into heaven, according to all I had been taught. By the skin of his teeth, as my mom would say. And that would have been enough for me. I would have felt grateful that God answered my life-long prayer that he would not die suddenly without a chance to grasp this faith.

The miracle we *did* witness, however, far exceeded anything I ever thought to ask God to accomplish. We saw this love for people just well up in dad and spill out of him as he thanked the nurses who cared for him and the members of Pastor Lloyd's congregation that sort of took him under their wings. We witnessed a peace in his countenance that defied explanation as years of weight and guilt fell off his back, as clearly as the physical pounds he lost during his hospital stay. A transformation occurred that could only help the witnesses gain a better understanding of genuine redemption, something I do not think any of us could have appreciated so deeply before that time.

I was undoubtedly sad when my dad passed away and felt the profound loss as I grieved, but I also had this strange joy inside me that buoyed me along for a while. To outsiders, calling his *recovery* from sepsis a miracle was antithetical. He died, after all, right before he was able to come home, a tragic, untimely end. But in my estimation, the miracle of his physical healing was not the one that mattered as much as his spiritual rescue did, his conversion miracle. He *was* truly healed. My prayer was answered, and I felt seen by my Creator. Confident that God was real because this could not have happened otherwise. God had, indeed, heard praying as I lay on my bed many nights in the past. Ah, "The God Who Sees." Long ago, at church one night, I heard a visiting apologist say, "Our lives should raise questions for which only God is the answer." This life event is one of those case in points, and I have filed away that adage for just such occurrences.

Could it be that I was placed into this family for this very reason? To witness Norm Giuseppe's redemption? Or even better, to play a part in it? Thank God we had brought my dad to the better hospital that night we were forced into a quick decision. When dad recovered, he affectionately referred to me as his personal doctor, and he believed it too. That phrase, "you were made for such a time as this" resonates with me. When questioning my purpose, I sometimes play that refrain.

Though The Lord works outside of our timeline, when He knit me together in the beginning, He knew of this moment, this event. He knew what Norm would need to draw him to his knees before his Creator. God used me to lead my dad to Pastor Lloyd and ultimately to his Lord. His Rescuer. God certainly didn't *need* me in this feat, but maybe He knew my dad did. In His great mercy, He allowed me to be in this place. In this family. The daughter of Norm Guiseppe. My dad's doctor.

Is this the light I am meant to see as I am trudging through that cave? I must come out of the darkness. I feel the pull.

35

Exceedingly More

I can no longer keep this story behind glass like my old hard cover fairy tale book, refusing to let people touch it. Books are meant to be experienced. Stories are meant to be heard. I remember a teacher explaining that when we delve into reading, we live vicariously through protagonists. Readers escape their present reality by traveling through time and space in a novel. Sometimes we learn something fresh in an experience we could never encounter in real life. And other times, we so deeply empathize with a character because the experience is raw, familiar, authentic.

My private high school offered specialized English courses, and I delighted in a Shakespeare class where we studied tragic flaws significant enough to take down kingdoms or to cause a man to go mad with jealousy or sorrow. At age sixteen or seventeen, I realized that these stories, while made-up dramas, uncovered truths in the human condition. And, likely, in fulfillment of my English teacher's dream, Lear's suffering and grief roused in this student overwhelming emotion. Poor King Lear's plight was real to me. He loved his youngest daughter dearly and would give her his kingdom, yet she would not play the game with her sisters and flatter her father in a fake display of affection to win some contest of who loves him most. No such contest existed for me and my father. I remain thankful that we never held back words. My father never doubted my love for him, and I never doubted his for me. Our last words ended with our hearts' declaration, "I love you, Honey." And I had always felt he, indeed, gave me his kingdom. And I cannot hide that treasure that is still mine to cherish.

But we readers must accept that a metaphorical scalpel might lay our emotions raw as we experience these narratives. In truth, we all find ourselves in stories. Should I prevent someone from opening a similar wound to mine, making it impossible to clean it out and allow it to heal? My story might inspire someone to check for the menacing lump and get it removed before the cancer spreads throughout the whole body. These days, due to the increasing popularity of DNA testing, more and more real-life protagonists are finding those so-called skeletons in their families' closets. How many marriages survive such an explosion? How many people are broken by the revelations and cannot find the remedy? How many of us question who we are after light illuminates the broken genetic chain?

I have always theoretically dabbled in all things medicine. I thought briefly about medical school but let my fear of higher-level math keep me in what I thought the safer field of education. But after both of my parents' extended hospital stays, I grew quite comfortable discussing the terminology around disease, procedures and treatments with the physicians who were willing to go into detail. Once they saw my interest, they let me perform some of the tasks from which most family members shy away. And as I said before, I know the proper method of dressing an open wound and can steel myself against reacting to especially angry ones. I must now bandage up this festering injury, stitch my own fractured heart back together, and trust my skills to move on to recovery.

And then, I must bear witness to the cure. Help others answer that nagging question: Who am I really?

The father who nurtured me helped mold me into the person I am today. He is also a part of who I always was. I have heard people over the years iterate the old adage, "blood is thicker than water," thinking the cliche reinforces some great truth and comfort in times of trouble. When push comes to shove and people suffer hurt or break-ups, your family, your blood, always stands as the strong link that cannot be broken by circumstances.

I have never found this comforting, for I have cultivated friendships with people who feel like brothers or sisters. Indeed, my friend Amy's mom was like a second mother to me growing up. My husband and I have spiritual mentors who feel like aunts and uncles handing us beautifully wrapped jewels of wisdom that come from another realm, and we trust them with our lives. My dissatisfaction with the maxim lies mostly with the fact that my dad would be the "water" in the metaphor. My blood, my genetic links are stronger than the father I knew? Not even close.

During those years when I thirsted, like every child does, for time, for nurture, for guidance, Norm was the one doling out glasses of water, quenching my thirst. And water is life. Yes, this other man's blood flowed through my veins, but the water is what kept me alive. Sustained me.

Additionally, I learned that the origin of that irksome phrase we use today is quite the opposite of what we have come to believe. An old proverb from ancient cultures posited that "the blood of the covenant is stronger than the waters of the womb." Since a covenant is actually *cut* between two parties to seal the bond, blood is spilled. Hence, the term *blood brothers*. To emphasize how binding the covenant is, the saying meant that the choice in making that pact was stronger than brothers born of the same mother. The family you choose is stronger than your genetic family.

If God formed me originally, isn't He able to re-form me now? Way back in the beginning, in ancient scripture, when God calls Moses to a situation Moses doubts he can handle, God asks him a question: "Is anything too difficult for Me?" And soon, God establishes a covenant, a binding agreement, with Moses.

I feel like a small tree that has been pruned. Branches with green leaves have been cut off on both sides, and a bare stalk remains, standing there unable to point in any direction. The structure looks like a hopeless cause; passersby would say, "It's not going to come back." But we know from science, and from experience, that pruning is necessary. Some trees survive the most horrific fires and still bloom magnificently after the crucible. This tree *will* bloom again and will even display a fuller range. I can hear the doves whistling from the branches, hidden by new, green, budding leaves nearby.

Who am I to complain about a revelation such as mine? There are worse family secrets I could have learned. I found out that my dad was not my biological father, yes. But all of my memories of him create a solid hedge around me, protecting me from intruders, just like the hedge of boxwoods back in my woods, hiding me from what existed on the outside of them. He was my father, and nothing changes that fact. He was the one on whom I imprinted as a newborn child, just like my mom's little ducks. He was the one with whom I cut a covenant. Perhaps I am engraved on one of those scars on the palms of his hands, comingled forever.

And that beautiful miracle that he experienced near the end of his life, and I had the privilege to witness, was far more than I had even longed for in all my prayers.

Sounds just like scripture playing out in reality—the promise that God is able to do exceedingly more than we ask or imagine. The Omnipotent showed me that it was not too difficult a task to accomplish, the saving of my dad, who was once a thorough God-hater. Why not hold onto *this* truth as my prize, for the joy over my dad's restoration is immeasurable. And that reality only shines a brighter light on those father/daughter memories that crystalize all around me, continuing to follow me as I age.

I keep finding new canisters in storage, and like the old home movies, these memories perform on the white wall in front of me. And, with the scent of popped corn and hot butter swirling around, the images bring laughter, not sadness, especially as the distance from learning the truth stretches on. I have looped back to the years before my dad's death. Before I knew of any family secrets. Before those secrets had any power to crush my reality. And I find myself sort of resting there, where God, my Father, put me. For His purposes.

I know that if I could see my dad now, he would look into my eyes as he always did, smile with his arms reaching out, and pull me into a strong embrace. I would smell his aftershave, and we would probably dance to a Dean Martin tune, "You're Nobody 'Till Somebody Loves You." And because he is the only one I could ever dance with, my muscles would remember how to follow his lead, just like riding a bike.

I almost said, the biology would not matter anymore. But this *is* sort of biological, for the assurance is seated deep within my cells. And I think cells have memory too. Maybe I mean the old DNA would not matter.

It seems the memories have stuck onto twisting strands that are stronger than the original DNA, a thicker, stickier twine that has wound itself into tight spheres bouncing around the nuclei of my cells. After having been stuffed inside, this thread has overpowered and subdued those old, weaker strands. The original braided with the adopted. This new, sturdier double helix was also formed by The Creator Himself, just like the initial building blocks of the spirals. All of these genes and experiences make me who I am, who I always was, and who I am meant to be.

And the words of one of Amy Grant's old songs I used to sing over and over, right to The Great I Am Himself, long before I even recognized their personal significance, begin to play in my mind:

"All I ever have to be is what You made me."

I have two fathers. And, strangely, one of them is *not* Jan but my Creator who formed me in the womb and placed me here on earth. I was born the youngest child of an Italian man, Michelle Giuseppe, and grew to realize that I am still my Father's daughter.

You who felt yourself so different from everyone but me

Remain the same

Hearts return from whence they came

Bottles, gardens, factories

Your work

Books, stereos, universities

My work

Heresies

Philosophies

You who were regarded as distant from everyone but me

Remain so close

Spirits come and go like ghosts

Traditions, doctrines, sins

Your hopelessness

Traditions, doctrines, sins

My forgiveness

Bondage

Freedom

You whose scarred hands that begged for holding held me

Remain almost tangible

Souls engrave a mark almost legible

Needles, tubes, machines--writhing

Your death

Hands, prayers, friends--breathing

Your life

Intercession

Repentance

You who planted for years in a ground that was me

Remain to toil

Gardeners leave seeds in fertile soil

Messages, whispers, lessons

Your teaching

Memories, visions, Dreams

My grasping

Inhabitation

Salvation

Hearts return from whence they came

Yet still remain

Acknowledgments

First, my heartfelt thanks go out to my family for inspiration, even to the ones no longer with me.

"I thank my God upon every remembrance of you."

I am grateful for SE Reid's editorial expertise and her advisement.

I appreciate my writing group for being the first listeners of my story, especially for Benn and Gwen for stepping right into this story and contributing so many hours of emotional feedback—for your encouragement, your questions and your tears. You have no idea what those tears meant to me.

Brian and Stephanie, you have helped me in this process more than you know.

I thank my friends for letting me include them—the Marys, Krissy, Amy. You are forever with me. And Mary, thank you for letting me bounce all those ideas off you. You were always ready to play along. To my first beta readers, Anne and Tammy, I trusted you with my secrets and you held them gently.

And to someone who has been a wonderful friend and mentor to both my husband and me—Doc, you have meant more to us than you will ever know.

Sara Dietz of *Fire & Feast Books,* you helped me not only with the many technicalities of this project but also with bringing it all to fruition, especially that beautiful cover design. *Thank you.*

NOTE: Chapter 31's mention of *The Molecular Biology of the Cell* can be found at the following link.

(https://www.ncbi.nlm.nih.gov/books/NBK26834/)

Afterword

In the years since I learned the results of my ancestry test, strength has poked through the soil like those early crocuses you see for just a short time in the spring. At times, I go for a walk and inhale those fresh scents and think, I am ready to talk about this openly with my family. Other times, a heavy, misty rain falls and washes those bits of confidence away.

I began writing my story immediately after testing to flesh out all the feelings swimming around the deep. I met with just two new relatives; one I continue to keep in touch with via texting. I have reached out several times to a nephew in the area, hoping for a chance to meet another half sibling, but the burgeoning conversations die off eventually. I think the nephew is afraid to tell his father, my half-brother, something that might tarnish the family's reputation. Or he thinks I might want something.

Telling friends has proved as difficult as telling my own family. Not because I feared that people would treat me any differently, but I refrained simply because once I spoke this truth, there would be no going back. Similar to an AA meeting where one would admit, *Hello, I am So & So, and I am an alcoholic.* In this case, I would have to say, *I am Michelle, and I am not who you have always thought I was.* Sometimes, I would just rather people not know. I stay in hiding, especially to those closest to me.

I am happy that I never had reason to investigate DNA testing while my dad was still alive. For him to know those results would have crushed me.

Undoubtedly, now that this book has gone out into the world, I will have to remove that mask. Sure, people will forget about the revelation after a time, but how I identify with my heritage, my past, has already begun changing, and I have been covering that up for several years now. I am not sure how to live without the veil.

Sometimes I tell myself that I'm concealing the truth to protect others from pain. Perhaps my family members do not want to experience the truth of their parents or grandparents coming to light. Perhaps they do not wish to rewrite the history they have memorized up to now. But that's probably my own rationalization.

The commercial depicting a man who always thought he was Irish now donning a Scottish kilt after DNA testing makes light of the weight of finding a surprise result in your DNA test, as if you simply change outfits. NPE groups ("Not the Parent Expected") welcome newcomers to their growing numbers daily. One of my former students piped up at a birthday party that, "Get this—my mom found out her dad is not her biological father." The small audience in her kitchen gasped. Another young man going through a divorce and arguing over custody of his 4-year-old daughter came to a crashing halt when his wife told him the little girl is not his anyway, and she can prove it. Yes, the support groups are well attended.

I may tip-toe into NPE groups with my story because we are allies in this search for identity. I know some stories of people's origins lie in a deeper valley than mine. One woman shared her discovery—that she was a result of rape, and her parents who raised her never told her that she wasn't their own planned child.

I think I was the result of some form of love, and this comforts me a little. However, I am aware that many are not able to hold onto such an anchor. We are still allies, though, no matter the circumstances. Members of a club we didn't choose. A support group that didn't even exist not very long ago. We share our stories in different ways, and some just sit with the story. And that's okay too. We understand each other in ways no one else can. None of us can be pushed to tell our story to the world. Mine just fell out of me onto the page, and now I hand it off for it to become what it will.

I have been climbing this mountain to get myself out of the weeds and brambles below, and on my way up, I found people at various points. When we exchanged stories, it felt like I grabbed onto their hands, and we helped each other hike the incline.

Perhaps that's what this book can do: grab someone on the way up. Show that there is One who can pull us from the miry clay and set our feet on solid ground. Breathe strength into our lungs from up top—clear oxygen—so that we can share our stories without fear of tumbling down the other side of the summit. Let's grab hold.

www.ingramcontent.com/pod-product-compliance
Lightning Source LLC
Chambersburg PA
CBHW061737120626
46550CB00005B/1817